THE MILLENNIUM:

WILL IT BE

INTRODUCED OR CLOSED,

BY THE

SECOND ADVENT?

WILL IT BE

PRECEDED BY A RESURRECTION OF THE JUST?

&c.

Being an Examination of the Main Arguments adduced by the Rev. W. LYON, B.A., against Millenarianism, in some recent Articles of the 'Evangelical Magazine,' now published under the title of 'Millennial Studies.'

BY

W. W. ENGLISH.

_____

PUBLISHED FOR THE AUTHOR BY

ARTHUR HALL, VIRTUE, & CO., 25, PATERNOSTER ROW, LONDON.

Price One Shilling.

1856.

THE MILLENNIUM:

WILL IT BE

INTRODUCED OR CLOSED,

BY THE

SECOND ADVENT?

WILL IT BE

PRECEDED BY A RESURRECTION OF THE JUST?

&c.

Being an Examination of the Main Arguments adduced by the Rev. W. Lyon, B.A., against Millenarianism, in some recent Articles of the 'Evangelical Magazine,' now published under the title of 'Millennial Studies.'

BY

W. W. ENGLISH.

PUBLISHED FOR THE AUTHOR BY

ARTHUR HALL, VIRTUE, & CO, 25, PATERNOSTER ROW, LONDON.

Price One Shilling.

1856.

PREFACE.

It is in no spirit of controversy that the writer would address himself to the impartial reader of Gods' word. It is under the full conviction, that the subject matter of the following pages involves a principal of the highest importance to all who profess to receive the Bible as alone authoritative in points of doctrine. When he thinks of the many exhortations to watch for the thief-like Advent of the Lord at an unknown and an unexpected hour, he cannot but feel persuaded, that every attempt to draw away the minds of the people from *present* watchfulness, is to say the least a circumstance of deep regret, and should have its counter influence from those who think so. The writer's opinion is not that men need any extraneous means applied to put away the duty of watching for their Lord, there is a sufficient tendency in the human heart of itself to do this, without needing any other incitive to effect a deeper sleep than alas prevails most generally in the minds of men, respecting the Second coming of Christ.

The writer has read with regret the varied shades of argument put forth in some recent articles of the 'Evangelical Magazine' to set aside the duty of watching for the Second Advent as *pre*-Millennial. These articles however having now assumed a permanent form under the title of 'Millennial Studies,' by the Rev. W. P. Lyon, B.A., the writer has felt it his duty to give such arguments in the main a somewhat brief consideration. With all due respect to their author, we would say, that the *Pre*-Millennial Advent was not as he very strangely and erroneously affirms, regarded by Paul as mistaken, nor did the Thessalonians ever receive at his hand, or from his lips any REBUKE respecting their views being the same as modern Millenarians hold! So that when we are told that—"Opinions similar to those of Modern Millenarians which sprang up (more properly,—flourished) in the Early Church," were *rebuked* by Paul, we beg to contradict the writer of 'Millennial Studies, and inform him, that such rebuke as the Thessalonians received leaves him *without* instead of—'*with* Apostolic example to justify him!'

Instead of finding a precedent for *his* rebuke, as he affirms in Apostolic times, we rather think he will have to seek for it in the allegorising system of the Alexandrine school, which sprang up in the *third*, instead of the *first* century! Strange indeed it would appear that 'Apostolic example' should not have produced any '*orthodox Christians*' earlier than the *third* century! And yet this must be so, if Mr Lyon is right and the early Christian Fathers are to be credited. Justin Martyr, Irenæus, Papias, Tertullian, Victorinus, Nepos, Lactantius, and other eminent Fathers of the *first*, *second*, and *third centuries*, were all *Millenarians*! Justin Martyr, says in the middle of the *second* century—"I and as many as are *orthodox Christians, in all respects*, do acknowledge the resurrection of the flesh, and a thousand years reign in Jerusalem restored, &c" appealing to Ezekiel, Isaiah, and the words of Peter (Acts iii. 21) as teaching such views! Burnet, after enumerating a long list of the early Fathers holding these views from John, up to the *fourth* century, says—"The christian doctrine of the Millennium, *was not called in question, so far as appears from history, before the middle of the third century!!* See "Burnetii Telluris Theoria Sacra" Bishop Newton too, speaking of this doctrine says, "The doctrine of the Millennium, *was generally believed in the three first and purest ages,* and this belief as the learned Dodwell hath justly observed, was one principal cause of the fortitude of the primitive christians, they even coveted Martyrdom in hopes of being partakers of the privileges and glories of the Martyrs, in the *first resurrection*"—(Dissertations, p 667) Strange indeed that those who enjoyed the benefit of John's *oral* teaching, and their successors for so many generations, should not have been *orthodox!* Strange indeed that *Post*-Millennialism, if true and apostolical, should be without an ORTHODOX supporter in the *three first ages* when the Church was *purest in doctrine!*

So far from making these Scriptural exhortations to watch, apply only in a practical sense to those who may chance to live some 1000 years hence, we would express our firm conviction that never was there a time, when they should be more seriously considered than now we live in times big with eventful issues Prophetical dates are running, or well nigh run out so far as man can tell the Jews are gathering homewards the blasted fig tree is beginning to bud and give forth signs of spring, which seems to tell us that summer cannot be far distant the Seventh Millenary of the world the great *Sabbatismos* (when Athanasius said—*the Lord would judge the Earth*) is fast approaching—Men too are spurning away from them the idea of their Lord's return, just the *Cardinal* trait of the times, according to *Apostolic* warning, when Christ shall appear These and a thousand other portentous signs of the times, all seem to remind us that we live at a responsible season Whatever specious arguments may be used to show the Apostles did not, or could not watch for the Second Coming of Christ as chronologically *near*, we are quite sure such specious arguments will not justify us in looking for him as chronologically *distant!* The command—'watch ye' was given because—'Of that day and hour knoweth no man.' And surely such command ought to come down to us with an accumulated weight of responsibility—'On whom the ends of the world are come.'

As there are two important passages of Scripture Mr Lyon has criticized—Acts iii 19, 21, and Matt xxiii 38, 39, we have omitted noticing for want of space—we just glance here at his argument upon the first, and observe respecting the second—that the very passage he quotes in support of his '*spiritual*' view, Matt xvi 28, upsets it—for instead of referring to a *spiritual* seeing as Mr Lyon states on the day of Pentecost—it referred to a '*personal* seeing' about eight days after in the Mount of Transfiguration! Acts iii 19, 21 This passage applied by Millenarians to the *Pre*-Millennial Advent, Mr Lyon has met by an extract from Faber's 'Sacred Calendar of Prophecy' Mr Faber quotes from ancient authorities and says the 'well judging' ancients, among whom he mentions Irenœus, confirms his views It is however quite plain the Ancients were only 'well judging' in his estimation here, so far as he could make them speak his own views Irenœus was a Millenarian, and Justin Martyr contemporary with him quotes these very words of Peter in this passage to prove the Millenarian doctrine! But we will put the argument of Messrs Faber and Lyon here to the test, it may be expressed thus—'*All* the *things* of which the Prophets spake are to be accomplished *before* Christ leaves heaven hence the Millennial era of which Daniel, Isaiah, &c. spoke must *precede* the Second Advent.' The true rendering of the passage ought to have saved Messrs Faber and Lyon from the egregious blunder they here fall into —"Repent ye therefore and be converted ... .And he shall send Jesus Christ, which before was preached unto you, whom the heavens must receive, *until* the *times* of restitution of all things, of which *times* (not of which *things*)God hath spoken by the mouth of all his holy Prophets since the world began " The meaning is plain The heavens retain Christ, *until* the *times* shall come, of which the Prophets spake—viz the times of universal peace and righteousness, succeeding the 'time and times and a half' of Daniel, and those epochs which precede the universal and everlasting kingdom of Messiah, or when the *New* covenant (Jer xxxi. 31 and Heb viii 8--13) shall be made We do not here express our opinion upon the view— "that we are now under the 'New *Testament*' dispensation of the '*Old* Abrahamic Covenant," but only introduce it as held by many eminent men, and which sweeps away at one blast this argument, and indeed the whole *Post*-millennial hypothesis But '*all things* of which the Prophets spake *precede* the Second Advent.' The plain statement of Daniel, that the Son of Man comes *at the setting up* of the Millennial Kingdom, we here for the sake of argument pass over and observe,—that if the Second Advent *succeed,* instead of *precede* this *Everlasting* Kingdom, it will be *postponed for ever!* Again, '*All things* of which the Prophets spake, *precede* the Second Advent;" so say Messrs Faber and Lyon. Then Isaiah speaks of 'new heavens and a new earth' (lxv 17, and lxvi 22) hence they *precede* the Second Advent!! But we turn to (p 131) of 'Millennial Studies,' and find Mr. Lyon writing thus—"St Peter thus agrees with St John in teaching us that the 'new heavens and new earth' will have no existence, *till after the Millennium and the Judgment!*" Is this not a *contradiction?* Is this not a *faux pas?* Does Mr. Lyon believe that Isaiah's 'new heavens and new earth' *precede* the Second Advent ; and also that the same spoken of by Peter and John, will have no existance *till after the final judgment* ! ! Where then does Mr Lyon carry the Second Advent to ?—*beyond the final judgment* ! ! Who then is the judge upon the ' great white Throne ?' Mr Faber has surely supplied Mr Lyon here with a fearful *Snare !* We must however award to Mr Faber the merit of making subsequently a tacit admission of his error here In the mellowed judgment of four-score years we find him thus writing. "From some Prophecies, particularly that contained in the last chapter of Zechariah (14, 4 !) no person can be blamed for expecting a *literal*, though only *temporary* manifestation of our Lord *on the summit of the Mount of Olives* ! !" p 49 "The Revival of the French Emperorship." Mr Faber then in his more matured judgment casts Mr Lyon's argument overboard, and mark the fact, this statement is made in connexion with the *final destruction of the papacy*, accompanied at least with a *temporary* manifestation of the Lord ! Mr Lyon's assertion that in no passage is ' Christ represented as coming for the destruction of the man of sin' would seem here to sustain a severe shock from his aged Friend ! Mr Faber's acknowledgment of a *literal* Advent in connexion with the destruction of the Apostasy *before* the Millennium, is nothing more or less than a renunciation of all those means employed to bolster up a *Spiritual* interpretation of such passages as 2 Thess. ii 8 ! To Mr. Lyon the example of his late Friend would seem to say—' Go thou and do likewise !'

We here make an additional observation or two upon Rev xix. 11, 21 The general imagery employed respecting ' The King of Kings and Lord of Lords' is very easy to understand. ' The sharp sword proceeding out of his mouth, and with which he will *Smite the Nations*,' must not however be confounded with other similar phrases meaning the preaching of the Gospel, but would seem more correctly expressed by John (xii. 48) ' The word that I have spoken, *the same shall judge him at the last day*.' The Gospel is preached as a witness to all, but it will prove to many a witness of condemnation. The great Slaughter doubtless refers to a *miraculous* interposition of God inasmuch as there is no account of any real battle fought only the preparation for it, and the issue of it. But we wish more particularly here to observe, a few things plainly inconsistent with a *post*-millennial hypothesis. 1 This miraculous slaughter is such as would lead us to reject any interpretation, that would not make it refer to God's day of vengeance and controversy with the nations, and connected with the Second Advent as plainly declared in the chapter 2 That part of this Judgment is *final*, no man can dispute, the Beast and False Prophet are at once and for ever cast into the lake of fire, *without passing through Death and Hades*, and this is plainly inconsistent with the idea that such should occur in the middle of this dispensation. 3 The idea of a *general* judgment after the Millennium, is here for ever crushed ! The judgment day being regarded either as a *brief* period, or entirely *post*-millennial, is here shown to be opposed to the plainest Scripture testimony It matters not whether the Beast and False Prophet be understood only as the ' *leaders*' of this confederacy, or whether as many hold ' *a body politic*,' they are at once and for ever consigned to their *final*, and unalterable abode, *before* the Millennium *begins*; consequently they cannot stand before the ' Great White Throne' on the supposition that it was set up *after* the Millennium had transpired ! This fact might have saved Mr. Lyon some trouble (p 131) about the judgment of Peter and John being alike *post*-millennial ! 4 This *pre*-millennial destruction of the apostacy in Daniel vii and Rev. xix we suppose every one will allow embraces the *Tares*; why then may not Matt. xiii 40, 42 *refer to the same period*? If it be objected that the latter refers to the *final* judgment, we reply so does Dan vii. and Rev xix ! ! That Dan vii 9, 11, is at least partially *final*, is here proved to a demonstration from John's statement of the same events, and as John does not say that he saw the ' Great White Throne' set up *after* the Millennium, but that he saw it then *existing*, the probability would seem, that it is the same as that upon which the ' Ancient of days' sat— The *Eternal Judge* is there seated, just as set forth Rev xx. 11—*The Books are opened* (I wonder what is the *Spiritual* meaning of this, disconnected with the day of judgment): and Saints minister in the assize, why then we ask again separate Dan. vii. 9, 11 from Matt. xiii. 40—42 ?

If we have touched here and there upon arguments used against Messrs Birks, Bonar, and Rees, it was only because of the important bearing these arguments had upon our main question and not at all with the intention of defending these writers, who are all well able to defend themselves, and give satisfactory replies to every shade of criticism to which their works have been subjected

The *pre*-millennial resurrection being so interwoven with the main point in the controversy, could not have been justly omitted, a few of the more prominent points in favor of its acceptation, have therefore been noticed, as telling the great and important truth, demanding the serious thought of every Christian, that of the Second Coming of Christ to *introduce* the Millennium.

September, 1856.

CORRIGENDA.

Page 6, line 18, for '100 years' - read '*more* than 100 years.'✱
  ,,   31, ,,   2, ,, 'John says' - ,,   '*Christ* says'
  ,,   39, ,, 33, ,, 'no information' ,,   'no *further* information.'
  ,,   63, ,,   5, ,, 'his body' - ,,   '*Christ's* body.'
  ,,   67, ,, 21, ,, 'It is' - - - ,,   'Is it.'

✱ GIBBON tells us from A.D 96,—the death of Domitian, through successive reigns to A.D 180, the Roman Empire was never so prosperous, only after this did Pagan Rome begin to decline, yet Mr. Lyon upon Zech. 14 makes '*the second verse*' refer to the siege of Titus, A.D 70 '*the third verse*,' refer to some time '*after*' A.D. 180 and '*the fourth verse*' refer *back again to* A.D. 70! And this is done notwithstanding the fact, that these verses are all connected by copulative conjunctions, and must all refer to the same period!

THE SECOND ADVENT.

THERE is not, perhaps, a question among Theologians in the present day, of greater popularity than the one we are now to consider, and we might add, that we think there is not a question among Christians, non-essential, that is of more importance. It has enlisted on both sides men of vast and respectful attainments, men whose names we revere, whose characters we admire—profound in learning—mighty in intellect—sound in judgment—and of inestimable piety. We would indeed shrink from a comparison of names, because we do not like comparisons;—not that we should be ashamed of our company on the *Premillennial* side; but because we think it would in no way serve the end we have in view—that of ascertaining " What saith the Scriptures " concerning the Kingdom and Advent of Christ. We would honestly then, but with all due respect to him from whom we beg to differ, express our firm conviction that Mr. Lyon has not given the world a fair exposition of " What saith the Scriptures " concerning the Kingdom and Advent of Christ; and to maintain our convictions upon this point, we propose to investigate some of the main arguments adopted by him, to set aside what we believe to be the truth. In proceeding then to notice those passages from which he infers the Postmillennial Advent, or rather those which he states do not teach that it will be Premillennial, we propose in the first place to notice a few of his arguments used to set aside the Premillennialist exposition of Zech. 14, &c., and the interpretation he has put upon such passages. The writer feeling satisfied of the entire fallacy of his interpretation of that and similar portions of Holy Writ, and of the arguments he has used to set aside the views of those who think differently from him, he thinks the impartial will be materially assisted by an investigation thereon, and enabled more correctly to judge of the soundness of his reasoning and views upon other points in the controversy.

We will quote in the first place a few verses of this chapter, more particularly bearing upon the point at issue. "Behold the day of the Lord cometh, and thy spoil shall be divided in the midst of thee, for I will gather *all* nations against Jerusalem to battle, and the city shall be taken, and the houses rifled, and the women ravished, and *half* the city shall go forth into captivity, and the *residue* of the people shall not be *cut off from the city. And his feet shall stand in that day upon the mount of Olives*, which is before Jerusalem on the East. And the Lord my God shall come, *and all his Saints with thee* And the Lord shall be king over *all the Earth*, in that day shall there be one Lord, and his name one. And men shall dwell in it, and there shall be *no more utter destruction*, but Jerusalem shall be *safely inhabited.*"

Mr. Lyon's interpretation in brief, is something like the following —the siege here spoken of is referred to the destruction of Jerusalem by Titus, 1,800 years ago. "The Lord going forth and fighting against those nations, &c., was fulfilled in the utter destruction of Pagan Rome.—(i e. 100 *years after this siege* !) "His feet shall stand in that day upon the Mount of Olives," is compared to a similar description, he says in Micah 1, 3, 4, "Behold the Lord cometh forth out of his place, and will tread upon the high places of the land, and the mountains shall be molten and the valleys cleft." "And the Lord my God shall come, *and all his Saints with thee.*" to Isaiah xiii. 3, 5, 7. "I have commanded my sanctified ones... They come from a far country, even the Lord . Behold I will stir up the Medes.. " Perhaps however, it is here added, the comment of Scott on this passage may be *nearer* the truth, "Christ would come to destroy Jerusalem, and to establish the gospel church, in which all his saints would joyfully concur." Such is in brief Mr. Lyon's exposition of these verses, in Zech 14. And I think it may here be added, that if such be our interpretation of prophecy yet future, and respecting the hopes of the church, the views we must have will be very *misty* and *obscure* indeed! First, we are to believe this siege was fulfilled in that of Titus, in the year 70. Then we are to believe that something less than *a tenth part* of the people spared at the siege of Titus, was the fulfilment of "*half* of the city shall go forth into captivity." We are to believe that about *a twelfth part* of the remaining half of the people spared at the siege of Titus, was the fulfilment of "*the residue* (remaining half) *of the city shall not be cut off.*" We are to believe

that *none remaining*,—the city *razed to the ground* (according to our Lord's pre-
diction in Luke xix. 43 & 44), at the siege of Titus, was the fulfilment of " *half
remaining in the city*, men dwelling *safely in it*; no *more* utter destruction, but
Jerusalem safely inhabited." We are to believe that *no appearance whatever of the
Son of Man*, was the fulfilment of " *His feet shall stand in that day upon the
Mount of Olives?*" No, this is compared to a description of Micah, which Mr.
Lyon says was fulfilled at the Syrian invasion! Then again, "The Lord my
God shall come and *all his Saints with thee*." This we are to believe means
something analagous to what was predicted in Isaiah 13, or all his saints and
angels joyfully concurring in the destruction of Jerusalem, and the establishment of the gospel church! Now such is Mr. Lyon's exposition of the passage,
and I should think no one can fail to see a manifest uncertainty about it; with
all due respect to him, I really think it is either *any* kind of exposition, or *none*
at all; he is evidently here unable to put any reasonable explanation upon it
apart from the common sense method of allowing plain and obvious declarations
to have their plain and obvious meaning. His exposition of the siege we have seen
is entirely misplaced, for instead of fitting with that by Titus in the year 70, we
have observed that it is at variance with it in *every particular*. It evidently has
reference to a seige that must yet be future, why then not allow the Lord's feet
standing upon the Mount of Olives, &c. to be future also,—and thus harmonize
with the the rest of Scripture! To object to such a reasonable exposition of the
passage on Mr Lyon's ground, because of other figurative phrases to be found
in the Bible, is exceedingly futile ; the safest way depend upon it, is to allow
God when he speaks, to mean what the language of the spirit conveys, always
and every where, unless such exposition would be doing violence to other re-
vevealed truths. In this instance the reverse is the case, for such exposition
harmonizes with other similar predictions unmistakably future.

But what, it may be asked, is our view of these verses. We hold as we have
said, this siege to be *yet future*. The feet of the Lord standing upon the Mount
of Olives, the place from where he ascended, and to where he will again descend,
as we are elsewhere informed, to be *yet future*. "The Lord my God shall come
and all his Saints with thee," instead of comparing it with Is. 13, with which it
has nothing to do, we compare it rather with such phrases as these, where
there is evidently a connection, 1 Thes. iv. 14 " For if we believe that Jesus
died and rose again, even so them *which sleep* in Jesus, *will God bring with him*."
Jude xiv. " Behold the Lord cometh *with ten thousand of his Saints*." 1 Thes.

iii. 13. " At the coming of our Lord Jesus Christ *with all his Saints.*"   It is a prediction of the *Coming of our Lord Jesus Christ with all his Saints,*—the living Saints changed and caught up, as Paul says, to meet him in the air, and the dead Saints raised—those that *sleep*—shall God bring with him.   And then we have afterwards Jerusalem "*safely inhabited*" by them, after the apostacy and destruction of the wicked are passed away , and subject no more to " *utter destruction.*" Instead of making this " safe habitation" refer to the *past*, when Jerusalem has been " *trodden down of the Gentiles,*" we compare it rather to the happy state of the Millennial era, when she shall be be free from foes without, and foes within, when there shall no more be learned the art of war, when " nation shall not lift up sword against nation ," when universal brotherhood shall prevail ;— and when " the Lord shall be king over all the earth, one Lord and his name one."   We think this declaration of the Prophet a great deal more like the Personal Reign of Christ upon the Earth with his Church, than any thing that has ever occurred *since* the siege of Titus.

Now the Rev. A A. Rees, of Sunderland, holding this siege to be *yet future,* and the other descriptions we have briefly gone over, as seen in a Pamphlet of his — " The Personal Reign of Christ on Earth demonstrated," has met with the most unsparing criticism here, which will furnish us with a sample of the mode of reasoning adopted, to set aside our interpretation of the passage. " This chapter' Mr. Rees says, ' is to be literally understood '   Let us see whether this be possible.   The Prophet says of the Messiah, " He shall grow up before him as a tender plant, and as a root out of a dry ground."   He is brought as a Lamb to the slaughter," &c.   Can these expressions (it is asked) be understood literally ? Will Mr. Rees tell us what is the *literal* meaning of " the travail of Messiah's Soul "?   Did he literally grow up as a tender plant ? &c., &c., page 154.   Mr. Lyon concludes from this kind of reasoning, that Mr. Rees' interpretation it must be evident even to a child, if applied throughout to this prophecy, would reduce it to absurdity!"   Now surely this cannot be intended to annihilate Millenarianism!   These criticisms are to no purpose whatever.   I am sure Mr. Rees never meant that such phrases were to be understood in any other than their common sense light.   If however, Mr. Lyon really means that in contending for a future siege, and a *literal* coming of the Lord as revealed in the chapter, he will bind us down to literalize *all* other passages, I should think the rationality of such reasoning will be difficult for any rational man to see.   Beside, if so, we must compel Mr. Lyon by the same Rule to *spiritualize all* other passages !   What *spiritual* meaning I wonder will he give to the following phrases in the same chapter he chose, Isaiah 53. "He is despised and rejected of men." "A man of sorrows and acquainted with grief." "He was smitten of God and afflicted." "Wounded for our transgressions," &c. If we are to literalize *all* in order to make good our views, then our brethren must spiritualize *all*, in order to make good theirs. Mr. Lyon, according to his manner of dealing with Mr. Rees, cannot be allowed to believe that all these predictions fulfilled to the very letter according to history, could have ever been so fulfilled ! Such reasoning indeed is a mere waste of words, it will serve no purpose in the cause of truth : we want to get at the truth ; and I am sure we none of us shall loose anything by finding it out. Why then contend thus ? Let us be honest, and set ourselves to work as if we wished to get at the mind of the spirit. Mr. Lyon has no more shown Millennarians to be wrong in their exposition, than he has succeeded in giving any thing like a reasonable interpretation himself of the passage.

I think Mr. Lyon has also wandered from the path of reason just as far upon Matthew 24. He must, I think differ from every Commentator, both past and present, in maintaining that the *entire chapter* relates to the destruction of Jerusalem and the dispersion of the Jews. He must be sensible of his error in maintaining this, he must feel satisfied of his objections being false, as seen in his rejoinder to Dr. Cumming's critique ; when the Dr. asks " If Christ came at the destruction of Jerusalem *like lightning* ?" It is objected that he cannot come " *like lightning* " at his Second Advent, because it is said in Acts i. 11, that he " shall come *in like manner* as he was seen go into heaven !" He cannot then come " *like lightning*," because of this passage in Acts. Beside it is said in verse 30, that he comes " *with the clouds*," consequently another insuperable barrier is again presented to Mr. Lyon in accepting of such phrases as referring to the . Second Advent ; " *lightning*," it is said, does not travel " *upon clouds* !" Hence he cannot come " *as lightning*," in the 27th verse ; and again, "*with the clouds*," in the 30th verse ; both cannot refer to the same event, because of this verbal difference ! I wonder if Mr. Lyon *can really* believe these following predictions referring to his " *First Advent*." " The seed of the woman shall bruise the serpent's head." Here we have included the idea of an oppressor. But then the same divine personage is again said to have been " led as a lamb to the slaughter." " Grow up as a tender plant." Here we have included the idea of meekness ; yea, the one phrase conveys the idea of a *subduer*, the other of *being subdued*. How can Mr. Lyon believe in both these ? Why it must be evident to every one if such objections as he has really made upon Zech. 14, and Matt. 24. are we to have any weight in our search after truth,—that we must give up the Bible altogether! Mr. Lyon according to his reasoning here, cannot believe in the genuineness of the Lord's Prayer, as recorded by the two Evangelists, because there is a *verbal difference* of expression! He cannot believe in Isaiah ix, 6 & 7, including the *idea of a Prince;* and Isaiah liii. which may be said to include the *idea of a beggar*, and yet both these he professes to believe as referring to the first Advent! Zech. ix. 9 & 10 is again not to be reconciled with Matt. viii. 20, and thus we might go on with such criticising until he would be left *without a Bible at all*. his position is seen to be false, not only because of such objections, but quite untenable in a number of instances,—for example, this 24th chapter he says refers *entirely* to the destruction of Jerusalem, but he is obliged, nevertheless, to make "the gathering of the elect" spoken of, *in it*, to refer to the gathering of the elect *then, since, and yet to be!* "The tribes of the earth mourning," is referred to the destruction of Jerusalem, although the same is predicted by John, in his Apocalypse, *written years after Jerusalem's destruction!* "His coming in the clouds," spoken of in verse 30, is referred to the same event, although the very same is referred to, and described in the same language by John, in his Apocalypse, written *years after*. "Of that day and hour *knoweth no man*," is referred to the destruction of Jerusalem, which was *clearly foretold* by signs, which, they *then* living, should see come to pass,—*knew* that the *desolation thereof was nigh*. Yes, all these descriptions of his Advent, relating to the question "What shall be the sign *of thy coming* and of the *end of the world*," are, strange to say, made to refer to the destruction of Jerusalem! These few notices of Mr. Lyon's dealing with his opponents, and mode of interpretation, • will suffice to show *how he has disposed* of Millenarian strongholds, and what *he thinks* "the Scripture saith concerning the Kingdom and Advent of Christ."

I shall now notice what he has found out and been pleased to call "*a Millenarian incongruity*." "We request," he says, "the attention of our readers to the following consequences that result in the supposition that the Millenarian hypothesis is the true one.—First, we have the *incongruity* already adverted to —that while 4,000 years were occupied in the work of preparation, for the *laying of the foundation stone* of the spiritual temple,—the temple itself *is reared in less than half that space of time*. It seems most anomalous that we should have such a *lengthened period* for the work, preparatory to the Saviour's First Coming,—and such a *brief period* for the development of all the results to be achieved by it, prior to his Second Coming." p. 117. Now in what light can we view this strange piece of argumentation ? What can really be said to it ? I would ask in the first place what is meant by the work of preparation *occupying* 4,000 *years*, the foundation stone of that spiritual house *only laid* after 4,000 years of our world's history *had passed away?* I seriously ask Mr. Lyon if he thinks *no stones were laid in that spiritual temple, before the First Advent of Christ?* What! the Patriarchs and Prophets all *refused* a place in that building! Abraham, Isaac, and Jacob! What then did our Lord mean, when he said *"ye shall see Abraham, and Isaac, and Jacob in the Kingdom of God*, and ye yourselves shut out." I never knew a christian man that did not believe this foundation Mr. Lyon talks about, *as being laid* 1,800 *years ago*, was laid *from all eternity*. See Matt. xxv. 34. "Come ye blessed of my Father, inherit the kingdom *prepared* for you *from the foundation of the world.*" Rev. xiii. 8. "And all that dwell upon the earth shall worship him, whose names are not written in the Book of life of the Lamb *slain from the foundation of the world.*" I marvel at Mr. Lyon's idea, —the foundation *only* laid when Christ assumed humanity. With all respect, I say, if the argument constructed upon this, to my mind, *unscriptural notion*, be worth any thing at all, Mr. Lyon must believe that not *one soul was ever saved until Christ hung upon the Cross*, to suppose otherwise, *virtually annuls* the force of the argument he has here constructed. If 1,800 years ago *only* this foundation was laid, why then it follows to a demonstration prior to that, *not one stone could have been laid in that vast superstructure*. It is necessary *first of all to have a foundation*, and this secured, *then only* can the building be carried forward, so that according to Mr. Lyon's argument here, we are to believe this spiritual temple only *began* to be built 1,800 *years ago?* Perhaps he will here tell us the superstructure in part was built *in vacuo*, and after 4,000 years of preparing this foundation were passed away, then this massive accumulation of spiritual stones were brought *ex vacuo*, and placed for the *first time in their proper places*! I now leave the foundation, and make an observation or two upon the builder. Mr. Lyon thinks he is *inconsistent* with himself—he has found out *an incongruity* in the management of his affairs; let us here invoke the arbitration of Paul to settle this disputed *inconsistency*. "Nay but oh man who art thou that repliest against God? shall the thing *formed* say to him *that formed it* why hast thou made me thus?" I wonder what Mr. Lyon has got to say about God *permitting* sin to enter Paradise, his *allowing* sin to remain in the world 6,000 years; his *casting away* of one nation and *calling* of another? And shall man indeed question the *seeming* disproportion of the affairs of His government, being *an atom* only himself in the great scale? I know Mr Lyon does not, I know he would not, but then the argument he has here constructed, is virtually doing so. But we would rather be disposed to think Mr. Lyon is *wanting* an opportunity to assail his brethren here,—we would rather believe that he is *without* Scripture to support him, and unable to find a *vulnerable* point in the views of his brethren His entire argument however, is annulled by the fact that, its base is not sound —not firm;—he has, we think, made a fearful mistake, in supposing the " spiritual temple " to have *begun* to be built *only* 1,800 years ago! when his views of that foundation are carried back to " *the Lamb slain from the foundation of the world,*" he is cut off from the merest shadow of strength, so far as his argument here is concerned.

But again, Mr. Lyon says in this chapter of his, " Christ has told us that the Father sent him not to condemn the world, but that the world through him might be saved," then he adds "the Spirit after 4,000 years have been spent in preparing for his coming to convince the world of sin, *fails in 2,000 years to effect this work.*" Such reasoning will satisfy no enlightened student of God's Word I think, nor shatter the faith of any Millenarian, nor the faith of any if inclined to Millenarian views. Christ did come to save, and not to condemn the world; but is it true that he will *not condemn the world because of that?* Mr. Lyon, I trust, will pardon my freeness here; but I really think his views of the present dispensation are anything but clear; the Bible must be to him a Book of confusion. We read in Acts xv. 14. that " Simeon declared how God at the first did visit the Gentiles *to take out of them* a people for his name " I dont mean by bringing forward this passage that God has not visited the Gentiles with the offer of salvation, so that they can *all* accept of it, but we have clearly taught the fact that *all* will not accept of it, that the present age is only a " *gathering together* of the elect, a taking out of those who will accept of the salvation offered them. Again, " This Gospel of the Kingdom shall be preached in all the world, *for a witness* unto all nations, and *then shall the end come* "; not preached to the conversion of *all*, but for *a witness to all*, an offer to all, so that all shall be without excuse. Christ indeed died for the sins of the *whole* world; but in no instance does he teach that *all* will be saved by that *universal* sacrifice. As he that offends in *one* point, becomes guilty of breaking the *whole* law; so the salvation of *one* soul required a sacrifice equal to the sacrifice required for *all.* God does not take account of sin upon this branch of the scheme of redemption, we think, in relative quantity; *one* sinner required the sacrifice that was made, *all* sinners require no more! The salvation wrought out by this sacrifice *has been* offered to *all*, *is* offered to *all*, and *will be* offered to *all*, but in no passage are we taught that *all* will accept of it; on the contrary, wherever the Second Coming of Christ is spoken of it is always associated with the idea of his coming to judgment, upon the rebellious *found living*, who have rejected him *to the last!* "There shall be mockers in the *last* times"! "When the Son of Man cometh shall he find faith on the earth"! He will find the world given up to worldliness as it was in the days of Noah and Lot! Tares and wheat *together!* But if Mr. Lyon contends for the opposite of this, as he would seem here, we ask what he means in his 4th Chapter, page 52, where he says— "When Millenarians, in reply to such reasoning, remind us that the Jewish People do not acknowledge Christ as their king, and that other nations still reject him, we at once admit the truth of this representation, but then we ask in reply, is not this the *predicted feature of His kingdom?* Was he not to rule *in the midst of His enemies*"! Then when Mr. Lyon is opposed in two ways can he use *first an electionist* argument to defend himself, and then again *an universalist* argument! Does he *now* tell us the design of this dispensation is to "*take out of them (the Gentiles) a people for His name*,"—*then* that the end of this dispensation will be the *conversion of all!* Can he believe both? What scripture does teach is, that the Gospel shall be preached in all the world, *for a witness*, and then *shall* the end come; and I ask if the efforts now put forth are not a *remarkable feature of the Times?* But again he proceeds—"Our main argument, in connexion with this branch of the subject, is the utter inconsistency of the conclusions to which the Millenarian Hypothesis conducts us with many most clear and positive statements of the Word of God It is evidently the Doctrine of Scripture, that the nations, instead of being destroyed, *are to be converted to God.* We admit, of course, that at the Coming of Christ there will be a *destruction of the ungodly*, but then we believe His Coming does not take place until the Gospel has *triumphed over all opposition*, and He reigns *throughout the whole world.* The destruction, moreover, according to our views, is the destruction of *an apostasy*; it is the destruction of those who, in spite of all the light which shone during the Millennial age, when the knowledge of the Lord covered the earth as the waters cover the sea, yet revolt from under the sceptre of Immanuel *and arm themselves for the destruction of His cause*"? Now really one does not know how to treat such a passage as this; this chapter, throughout

C

is a kind of inexplicable one altogether Mr Lyon would seem to be in a kind of undecided state of mind. We have first a belief that the Bible leads us to expect *the nations* to be converted to God; but then it is added,—Christ will come for the *destruction of the ungodly*! How can both these be true? But it is said further that he will not come until the Gospel has triumphed *over all opposition* and he reigns *throughout the whole world*! How then can he come for the destruction of *the ungodly*? To make confusion more confounded still, it is added, *this destruction* is the destruction of *an Apostasy*, and yet he comes when *triumphant* over *all opposition*,—the Gospel *universal*,—he reigns throughout the *whole world*! Yes, and beside, he comes to take vengeance upon some, who, in spite of Millennial light, revolt and arm themselves *for the destruction of the cause of him*, who has become *triumphant*, possessing a *universality* of dominion, without *disloyalty*! Can any man picture to himself views more confused— more incongruous—more opposed to each other? We feel compelled almost to think that Mr Lyon is in an uncertain state of mind, undecided what view to take, evidently so entangled in the meshes of a theory that he cannot speak out freely and take any decided view of Scripture truth , while he has been at the pains to show the world what he appears to have thought *" an incongruity"* among Millenarians; he has not only failed in the attempt, but actually exhibited himself, under the most *incongruous phases possible*!

We will now just glance at a few of his logical weapons employed against Mr. Birks, and, in the first place, I would remark, that upon the Personal Reign of Christ, yet future, I really think he has not even touched upon its point in his line of augumentation ; his quotations, so numerous, *only* prove that he now *spiritually* reigns, and this Mr. Birks believes just as truly and as fully as Mr. Lyon does himself he indeed contends that Christ does not now reign *de facto*, and so far, truly, as seen in Mr Lyon's *failure* in showing the contrary to be so. Mr. Lyon, indeed, has shown what Mr. Birks himself believes—that he now reigns *de jure*, and he has criticized the forms of expression used by that writer, to show what he thinks ought to be included in his reign *de facto* , but as far as Scripture is concerned he has not advanced one solitary proof of the contrary . he has not taken one step towards proving his reign, at present, being what is meant by those many passages which, we believe, to teach future *Personal Reign*. We believe indeed, in common with Mr. Lyon, that he has now a kingdom—that he now reigns—that he is now the Sovereign Ruler of all, but then he treats men as responsible creatures—he gives them now the option of accepting Him as their Sovereign—of suffering with Him *now*, that they may reign, *hereafter*, with Him in glory. We think our brethren do not allow that text to have its legitimate meaning. " The sufferings of Christ and the glory that shall follow." He suffered on Calvary, but His sufferings did *not end there*, he suffers *now* with each member of His mystical body. He was glorified when he finished the work appointed him to do, but then he was not *fully* glorified, He is not now, we believe, *fully* glorified, nor will he be until his sufferings shall be ended, and his glory completed ; when he shall come to be glorified in his Saints, and to be admired in all them that believe. We indeed allow that he now reigns, but he is yet in the " far country,"—he is yet " seeking" a kingdom—he has yet *to return.* We believe in that kingdom "which cometh not with observation." But we look for another *phasis* of that kingdom, which will one day come with "*outward show*"—when it will be unnecessary to say " see here, or see there," because the splendour of the King, in his return, will cover the horizon like the lightning glare which illuminates the darkest corners of the earth.

Mr. Lyon's reasoning upon Christ having *now* " all power" is really to no purpose whatever upon this point of disputation, it is sufficient to show the fallacy of such reasoning to observe that he has indeed *now* " all power," but then he had " all power " before *ever* this dispensation *dawned.* He, by whose word the heavens and the earth were formed—by whose *fiat* all things came into being—*ever had—will have* " all power." How futile then the attempt to show that he can admit of no increase by the addition of " David's Throne," the less being added to " David's Throne," the greater—the absolute—the all comprehending, the fact that he now has " all power," proves nothing in Mr. Lyon's favor, but rather militates against his entire argument, here, upon " David's Throne." Christ, when He ascended up on high and led captivity captive, it is argued *then*, became possessed of " all power," invested with *universal sovereignty !* We marvel at the blindness of such argument. What, He who *in the beginning* was the Word, and the *Word God*, did He then, 1,800 years ago, *only* become invested with *universal sovereignty ?* To what purpose is Mr. Lyon's argument here against Mr. Birks ? Again, upon the " Throne of David " yet to be possessed by Christ, it is asked, how can He, who now occupies the Throne of the *whole* world, receive, in addition to this, the Throne of a *portion* of the world. This, we are informed, would be enlarging the *universal,* by adding to it a *part of itself !* (Page 52) This then is to prove that Christ, since he was made the foundation stone of the spiritual temple (i.e. 1,800 years ago, according to Mr. Lyon), *then* became *absolute sovereign.* Now let us turn this logic round and view it in another light. Christ, who has *now* " all power "—who *ever had* " all power," it is contended—must have the " Throne of David " promised Him in that " *all,*" so that if this promise has been fulfilled *on this account*, it met with its accomplishment *before ever* it was *predicted !* Christ, in being promised the " Throne of David," strange to say, had that promise *fulfilled* before ever there *was a David*, or any *earthly throne established !* What then becomes of the promise ? Had it no meaning ? Mr. Lyon's logic virtually annuls it by taking up Christ's divinity to argue against promises made to him in respect of his humanity. What becomes of the meaning of the nobleman going into a far country " *to seek for Himself a kingdom ?* He ever had " *all* power." Could he then receive any addition to that " *all*" by the possession of the *part* he went to seek ? Mr. Lyon will answer this question. What becomes of such passages as the following, according to Mr. Lyon's reasoning—"All that the Father hath given me *shall come* to me." Could He, who now possessed *all*, receive any addition by the gift of a *part ?* See the fallacy of Mr. Lyon's weapons here. The same divine personage who said "*All* power is given to me, both in heaven and on earth," nevertheless could say " All that the Father hath given (not is *now possessed*) *shall come* to me." Mr. Lyon's logic here, if carried out would virtually annul every promise made to Christ in respect of his humanity, and he would be represented as possessed of, and ruling over the kingdom of darknsss !

We will now proceed to examine his argument upon the subject of the Second Coming of Christ not being Premillennial, which indeed is the key-stone to the whole arch. If we, therfore, find Mr. Lyon's reasoning, upon this point of the controversy, at fault, we may conclude that his book is an entire fallacy, without any Scriptural foundation or warrant, and based upon a mistaken notion of Holy Writ.

I quote a few sentences here from him respecting the Second Advent. " There is not in Scripture *a solitary passage* in which Christ in coming the second time, is represented as coming to *introduce* the Millennium or in other words, to reign upon earth," page 76. I observe before entering upon the investigation of his arguments to support this sweeping assertion, that my readers must be prepared to find Mr. Lyon very quietly *cutting away the personality* of Christ's Second Coming, wherever it is announced, and holding *in all their fulness* the blessings said to follow upon this fact ! I think this will materially assist the impartial in their " search after truth " to notice particularly, that in all the passages I shall adduce declaring that Christ will come to *introduce* the Millennium, Mr. Lyon receives all, or nearly all the *Millennial traits* attendant thereupon, but refuses to accept the *personal* Advent of Christ, which is just as clearly revealed in the Sacred Records.

But first a few words upon the assertion, that in no passage is Christ said to introduce the Millennium.   If by this bold sentence we are to understand that nowhere in a set number of words—verbally arranged in a given form, there is to be found a declaration of his Premillennial Coming, the answer would be— such a demand does not require to be fully met !   It is not, it never has been God's method of dealing with his intelligent and responsible creatures in such a way, that their intellectual powers should not need to be exercised . he does not treat man like an irrational creature , if he had given to him a revelation of himself—his works—and his ways, in such a manner that he could not by *any possibility* be led into mistake, why then he would have in a great measure destroyed his responsibility,—he would have precluded the necessity of exercising those powers of discrimination which he has endowed him with for the sole purpose of " *proving all things.*"   Such declarations of his *First* Coming were never given.   Why should we then be so unreasonable as to look for them respecting his *Second* Coming ?   The Jews erred upon this very point; they had in Is. 53, clearly enough revealed a Saviour suffering as preparatory to a Saviour reigning; but they needed to exercise their powers of discrimination to see this, and the absence of this led them into a fearful mistake—they looked for the crown without the cross—exaltation without humiliation—a kingdom of glory without a kingdom of grace as preparatory to that.   They looked for that kingdom which comes with splendour and pomp;—but they overlooked that kingdom which " cometh not with observation," which was to be its forerunner, made up of elements *not visible*, righteousness, and peace, and joy in the Holy Ghost.   Hence we see although the Messiah's two kingdoms one to " take out a people for his name," to gather in " all that the Father gave the Son ," and the other triumphantly to reign over the church complete, were both predicted clearly enough, yet men mistook the fact !   So now it may be, yea we feel assured it is so—that the glorious *personal* Advent of Christ declared in so many instances, as " coming to reign on the earth," is nevertheless overlooked or utterly rejected.   We have, as we shall now endeavour to show, in not a few cases, this great truth brought out clearly to a *demonstration*, while it is to be gathered from a hundred different passages in their sequence and dependence upon each other just as clearly, but we shall confine ourselves to those passages which we believe to teach it *literally and demonstrably.*

See Daniel vii. 13 and 14. "I saw in the night visions, and, behold, one like the Son of man came with the clouds of heaven, and came to the Ancient of days, and they brought him near before him, and there was given him dominion, and glory, and a kingdom, that all people, nations, and languages, should serve him   his dominion is an everlasting dominion, which shall not pass away, and his kingdom that which shall not be destroyed." I think we have in this passage contained a thorough refutation of Mr. Lyon's assertion—"that in no passage is Christ said to come and *introduce* the Millennium" In the first place, this passage either teaches his first coming or his second, it either teaches the establishment of Christianity, or it teaches its perfection; it either refers to the kingdom of grace, or to the kingdom of glory—Which? To maintain his ground, Mr. Lyon must believe it refers to the *First* Advent—the *establishment* of Messiah's kingdom of grace in the world, and is *now* in existence! Let us then briefly and unbiassed by systematic notions, examine the passage and see whether this view be not utterly untenable —Daniel sees a vision of four beasts, which are said to denote four *successive* Empires or Kingdoms; the first refers to the Babylonian empire; the second refers to the Medo-Persian empire; the third refers to the Macedonian empire, the fourth refers to the Roman empire. Upon all these Mr. Lyon will join in with us   Now this vision runs on to the time when Daniel sees another empire set up—the fifth in this series—that of the Messiah   the fourth is broken to pieces and consumed unto the end—*that the fifth may be set up*, which shall not, *like its predecessor*, be broken to pieces, but endure for ever ·—"this dominion is an everlasting dominion, which shall not pass away, and this kingdom that which shall not be destroyed." Then we have here to a *demonstration* the fact that this kingdom is *not yet set up*, because the fourth, its *predecessor*, is *still in existence!* and this coming of the son of man and *consequent* kingdom, must refer to a period *yet future;* so that we have here the Personal Advent of Christ to *introduce* the Millennium, or set up his kingdom, as clearly revealed as words can really make it! There is no getting over this passage, it cannot with any consistency be made to refer to the *first* Advent of Christ by any means, because then the *fifth* kingdom *in succession,* which is said to be founded upon the *ruins* of the fourth, its *predecessor;* would be made to exist *while* the fourth did! and not only so but actually *set up*, before the fourth had *reached its meridian!* The Roman empire was only *ascending* its meridian when Christ came to make an atonement for sin, hence the fallacy of applying this prophecy to the first Advent, is utterly ridiculous. Again we ask, how can the fourth be said to *exist* at the same time as the fifth—that of the Messiah, which is here said to be *universal and eternal!* Surely Mr. Lyon's logic about the *all* comprehensible, swallowing up the *limited* part of that *all*, must come down here upon those who hold that this kingdom is *already* set up, with crushing severity. Beside, that this kingdom has never yet been set up is manifest, from the 20th verse, where it is said, that a part of the Roman empire in its divided state (the apostasy) makes war with the saints, '*until the time came* that the saints possessed the kingdom.' This part of the fourth empire which has apostatized from the true faith, is *now* waging war with the saints, and hence we have *demonstrably* taught the fact, that this prophecy is *still to to have* its fulfilment! Again there is the " Babe born in Bethlehem," to be reconciled with the " Son of Man coming in the clouds—His *universal* reign over *all*, to be reconciled with his reign over a very *limited portion* of the human race! In fact, there is no foundation whatever for applying this prophecy to any other but the Millennial reign of universal righteousness and peace, *yet future;* and this appears to be Mr. Lyon's own view of the prophecy, for he says the " Ancient of days " is *now* sitting upon the apostasy to consume it, and thus make way for the kingdom of the Messiah ! Why, then you say he allows, at least, in one passage, that *Christ does come to introduce the Millennium*! He does virtually *demonstrate* this fact, but at the same time he denies it! He allows the whole prophecy to refer to the Millennial era, but *refuses to admit of the Coming of the Son of Man !* just what I wished my readers to be prepared to find, he will *have the kingdom* in all its universality—in all its eternity, but he *wont have the King !* Is this reasonable ? Is it fair ? Is it true ?

Let us now endeavour to sift Mr. Lyon's means employed to justify himself here. It is evident, from the inspired comment contained in the latter part of this chapter, he says that the vision, narrated in the preceding part, is entirely symbolical the four beasts represent four kingdoms opposed to the cause of God; the sitting in judgment of the Ancient of Days predicts the judicial visitations by which these kingdoms were to be destroyed. The Coming of the Son of Man to receive a kingdom, &c., *will be* fulfilled, not in any *visible* coming, anymore than the sitting of the Ancient of Days was fulfilled in a *visible* session of the Father. (Page 78.) Such then are Mr. Lyon's reasons for refusing to accept of a *visible* Personal Coming of the Son ! Entirely *symbolical*, he says, these beasts or images employed to represent the four kingdoms. What *image*, I wonder, employed, could be anything else but *symbolical?* Can an image or figure of representation be shown to be the *thing signified?* When Mr. Lyon *can* show this to be the case, he will then have some reasonable objection here to make ! Again, the Coming of the Son, here spoken of, will not be fulfilled in any *visible* Coming, any more than the session of the *"invisible"* Father (whom no man hath *ever seen*, or *can see*) was fulfilled in a *visible* sitting of the *"invisible"* Father ! Really, I think, every one must here say that Mr. Lyon is quite astray from that which has even the appearance of *rationality !* I think he must have overlooked the *"impossibility"* of his objections here ; he cannot mean this to be *"*challenging Millenarians to produce a solitary passage, which *clearly* refers to Christ's Second Coming, from Old or New Testament, in which the conversion of the world and His universal reign are represented as resulting from it ! (Page 79.) If indeed this reasoning be to make good such a challenge, why, then we at once concede the point, and allow that we cannot produce one solitary passage, for such objections as Mr. Lyon has made here to the doctrine of a *visible* Coming of the Son, in this passage, are utterly *impossible* to be met. They can only be overcome when an *impossibility* can be shown to be *possible !* If a "figure of representation" has to be shown to be that which it is intended to represent ; and if the *visible* appearance of the Son is to be demonstrated *only* when the *invisible* Father can be shown to be *visible*, why we will give up our point and allow that we are in error ; but I seriously ask Mr. Lyon, if he really meant these points of his argument to be valid, if they are likely to assist him in his "search after truth," *in finding it ?* Such objections are tantamount to saying, that he will not accept of a *visible* personal Coming of the Son upon *any* conditions. They require a miracle to overcome them—a reversion of the laws of nature ! Mr. Lyon is here then clearly seen to be *against* both Scripture and reason ; and so far as his argument is concerned, he is shown to have been in error when he said " in no passage is Christ said to come to *introduce* the Millennium," for we have here that great truth clearly taught, and he seen unable to offer one *reasonable* objection to its plain literal acceptation !

The same truth we have seen taught by Daniel is also clearly unfolded by John, in his Apocalypse, chaps. 19 and 20. We have a description of the Coming of the Son in the clouds of heaven, upon a " white horse," (the symbol of victory), the judgments descend upon the apostate nations,—the same part of the Roman Empire, in its divided state, we have seen mentioned in Daniel, as "waging war against the saints,"—the guilty nations are overturned, amid a vast slaughter of their subjects; and then we have the resurrection of the righteous, and their reign upon the earth with Christ—" they lived and reigned with Christ a thousand years." But to make good our belief here, we are again requested to accept this "white horse" *literally*, if we accept "the Son of Man" *literally*. That is an *irrational* objection put in to exclude what to say the least *may be possible*. Our brethren, we think, are far astray from that which can be deemed reasonable, in endeavouring to maintain their ground upon such a basis. No man ever did, or ever will, I should think, accept this "white horse" in any other than its obvious, *symbolical* meaning. However, if we are again compelled to meet our brethren upon their own conditions, we would ask if they are prepared to accept of those men, said to embody the principles of the Martyrs (their first resurrection) *figuratively*. It seems to us that consistency ought to compel them to make their first resurrection—spiritual reign of Christ, and His saints alike *spiritual—intangible*. We can, consistently, hold the "white horse" to be *figurative*, and the "Son of Man" to be *literal*, because such acceptation of the passage harmonizes with other portions of Holy Writ, and does not seem contrary to reason; but that the "*first resurrection*" should be maintained as *spiritual*, and the reign of Christ as *spiritual*, and yet be said to be materialized by living *corporeal* men, does seem, not only opposed to the Bible, but quite *antagonistic* to reason. We think then that Mr. Lyon is seen to be in error, in his argument about the "white horse," and quite incapable of offering, here *again*, any satisfactory reason for refusing to accept of a *literal* Coming of the Son of Man.

The same great truth we have seen taught also in Zech. 14. A Personal Coming of the Son to *introduce* the Millennium! Then we have his Personal Reign on the earth. "The Lord king over all the earth, one Lord and his name one." Just Christ living and reigning with his people, as taught by Daniel in his 7th chapter, and by John in the 20th chapter of the Apocalypse. Strange to say, in all the passages Mr. Lyon has selected and placed in juxtaposition to prove the *reverse* of this, the same truth is uniformly intimated or declared : we have him coming to take vengeance upon his enemies,—the rebellious nations *found living;* which proves that his coming will be at the *opening*, and not the *close* of that happy period ! they teach nothing about the Postmillennial idea of

D

a *general* judgement, for the righteous and wicked, dead and living, *contemporaneously ;* but the Premillennial view of the wicked *found living* only judged ! the wicked *dead* do not rise for judgment until a thousand years *after* this !

We will now advert to the famous passage in 2 Thes. ii. 1-8, which is allowed even by Mr. Lyon to have considerable strength ; and as it is considered by all to be one of the most knotty props of Premillennialism, we shall examine every shade of argument the writer of "Millennial Studies," has brought forward upon it, to set aside our views. We will quote as many verses as are necessarily bearing upon the point at issue.—"Now we beseech you, brethren, by the coming of our Lord Jesus Christ, and by our gathering together unto him, that ye be not soon shaken in mind or be troubled, neither by spirit, nor by word, nor by letter as from us, as that the day of Christ is at hand. Let no man deceive you by any means for that day shall not come, except there come a falling away first, and that man of sin be revealed,—the son of perdition... For the mystery of iniquity doth already work · only he who now letteth will let, until he be taken out of the way : and then shall that wicked be revealed, whom the Lord shall consume with the spirit of his mouth, and shall destroy with the brightness of his coming."

We think we have here again in this passage *literally* and *demonstrably* taught the glorious truth of the Second Coming of Christ to *introduce* the Millennium. In his first Epistle he says (v. 2 & 3), "For yourselves know perfectly that the day of the Lord so cometh as a thief in the night ; for when they shall say peace and safety, then sudden destruction cometh upon them and they shall not escape." The Apostle here informs, or reminds the Thessalonian Christians of the great fact, that the Lord would come "as a thief in the night," sudden— unexpected by the world,—just when they should be least expecting it, saying "peace and safety,"—*then* "sudden destruction cometh upon them, and they should not escape" ! This solemn announcement evidently alarmed some who need not have so feared : some of the weaker and more diffident disciples of their master, who doubtless often thought within themselves that they could hardly be reconciled ; they were of little faith, needing an increase : and consequently the stern announcement of the Apostle's respecting their Master's surprisal and dispensation of judgments upon the careless and unconcerned, produced in their minds no small degree of fear, they became alarmed for their own safety. But this was not evidently the impression the Apostle intended to convey,—he knew that "the day of his Coming" was wrapped up in much *uncertainty,*—he knew that the "mystery of iniquity" did then already work, and that it might be for aught he knew definitely respecting the "times and the seasons," soon reach its climax; and under the full conviction of the importance of ever keeping the mind intent upon that 'blessed hope,'—the glorious appearing of their great God and Saviour Jesus Christ—ever looking—waiting, and watching for his return; he told them that he would come *suddenly* like the flash of lightning, giving no visible signs of its approach, until the whole horizon should be lit up with one vast glare! And such indeed being the case, we see the propriety of the Apostle's timely warning, and kindly remembrance of such event: but as we have already observed, it was received by some among them to their own mental discomfort, and which perhaps was in some degree augmented rather than appeased, by others among them of stronger courage, and more confirmed in the faith, anxious for his return;—hence the Apostle's better judgment, who knew well the propriety of feeding such disciples with meat proportioned to their strength, was needed; and in his second letter he again takes up the subject by way of comforting such, and gives them such information as was sufficient to allay the fears of the timid respecting that event.—" I beseech you, brethren, concerning the Coming of our Lord Jesus Christ, that ye be not soon shaken in mind, *nor troubled*, neither by spirit, nor by word, nor by letter as from us, as that the day of Christ is at hand... Let no man deceive you, for that day shall not come except there come a falling away first (the Apostasy), and that man of sin be revealed, the son of perdition; whom the Lord shall consume with the spirit of his mouth, and shall destroy with *the brightness of his Coming.*"

The Apostle now endeavours to check this unhappy gloom set in upon these timid disciples, and beseeches them not to be so soon shaken in mind or troubled, that the day to which he had referred could not take place, *until* the "mystery of iniquity" then at work, should become fully developed; and then it would be "consumed by the spirit of his mouth, and destroyed by the brightness of his coming." What intelligent reader of God's Word would say here (supposing he knew nothing of the difference between Theologians upon the point we are now to consider), that we had got away from the subject introduced by the Apostle in the first verse of the chapter—his *personal return?* No man could gather such an idea unless *taught* to believe, that this last verse was intended to teach *another kind* of coming, We have in this chapter the great Antichristian Apostasy stated as stretching right on from the days of the Apostle, to the period when its destruction should be accomplished by the *"brightness of his coming."*

Mr. Lyon indeed does not deny that he referred to his *Personal* Advent in his first Epistle; he does not deny that he referred to the same great event in the beginning of this chapter in his second Epistle; and as there can be no Millennium *intervening* between the time of this apostasy in the Apostolic days, and the period to which the Apostle referred, when he said, it should be "destroyed by the brightness of his coming," we have clearly again *demonstrated* the fact of a *Pre*millennial Advent—the Second Coming of Christ to *introduce* the Millennium! Indeed Mr. Lyon does not believe between these bounding periods of the apostasy, that we shall have the Millennium; he does not believe that Christ and Antichrist will] reign together during that happy era; but fully allows of the apostasy being removed, to make way for the *Universal* Reign of righteousness and peace! Well then, I can fancy my readers saying secretly to themselves—he must be a *Premillenarian*! A believer in the great *Scriptural* truth of Christ coming to *introduce* that happy period! No, *as before,* he is willing to accept of all the Millennial traits he can, with the exception of the " *brightness of his coming* "! he will rejoice at the fall of the evil one, at the triumph of Christianity; but not at "the Advent of Christ" herein declared! spirituality, symbolicity, again is the reason; no *personality* connected with *this Coming* !

Let us now enquire upon what ground this is attempted to be done and justified. The whole of his argument apparently rests upon the *former* part of this 8th verse, being *figurative ,* "whom the Lord shall consume with the spirit of his mouth." If we regard the *former* part of the verse in a *figurative* sense, upon what principle it is asked can we interpret the *latter* part *literally ?* Surely this would be no uncommon thing for any Commentator to do. If our space would allow us we could give examples I think, sufficient, from Mr. Lyon's own class of interpreters, to show the utter fallacy of such an interrogation! We will take the first verse of Isaiah 53, a chapter to which we have before referred. " Who hath believed our report, and to whom is the arm of the Lord revealed." Mr. Lyon does not, I should think, disbelieve in the *literality* of the "Prophet's report" —i.e. that he *literally* made a proclamation! but does he believe in the *literality* of the " Arm of the Lord being revealed "? i.e. that he *literally* stretched out a *material* arm! Of what force then is his interrogation —" How can we interpret the *former* part of this eighth verse *figuratively,* and the *latter* part *literally ?* " Are we to put aside discrimination in deciding what is figurative and what is literal? Are we not to use our judgment? If such a principle be to actuate our interpretations, where shall we get to? We must *end* evidently just as we *begin ;* if we begin with Genesis *literally,* so we must continue right on without intermission to the end of Revelations! The force of such interrogation in itself considered, is seen to be utterly worthless! Had the former declaration in his first Epistle been interpreted *figuratively ;*—had the same event spoken of in the first verse of this chapter been maintained as *figurative ;* had the whole context been held as referring to a *spiritual* and not a *personal Coming ;* why then there would have seemed to be something like a shadow of reason for refusing here in the 8th verse to accept of a *literal* Coming! but no, this former declaration in his first Epistle, is allowed to be *literal,*—this second chapter in his second Epistle is allowed to begin with reference to the same *literal* advent—the *whole* context is allowed to refer to the same *literal* and personal coming ; but when he brings the subject down to the destruction of the apostasy by " the brightness of his Coming," and consequently the *opening of the Millennium ;* why then it is a *figurative* form of expression! a mere "*passing allusion,*" introduced *incidently ! parenthetically !*

But again, this Coming, in the *latter* part of the verse, seems to be maintained on the ground of *consistency.* The *former* part being figurative, so must the *latter* part also be figurative. Consistency requires *this,* although this *former* declaration in his first Epistle, and the *whole context,* we have just referred to, *may be ignored !* Is this consistency? Is this to be called either a safe or a sound principle in exegesis? Upon what principle, I ask, can Mr. Lyon believe in the *literality* or *personality* of the *whole* argument and context, and then without any break or digression from the subject of his *Personal* Coming, believe the Apostle in this verse only meant his *Spiritual* Coming? How can he believe (παρουσια) in the *first verse* of this chapter refers to his *Personal* coming, and without any digression from the subject of that Coming, when he uses precisely the same word in the *eighth verse,* can he believe that he refers to his *spiritual* Coming? How can he believe this *declaration,* in the *first* verse to be *literal ;* and the *accomplishment* of the same, spoken of in the *eighth* verse, to be *figurative ?* How can a man believe a prophecy to be *literal* and yet contend for a *spiritual* accomplishment? Yet this Mr. Lyon professes to believe,—he contends for two *opposite* kinds of fulfilment of the *same prediction ?* He has made no effort to prove that this verse refers to anything else but the *same event,* spoken of in the *first verse ;* he has not adduced any shade of argument to show that the Apostle here digressed, or left off from the subject he introduced with the chapter, but rests the whole of his argument here, apparently, upon what we have before-named,—" the *former* part of the verse being *figurative* " ! and because he says " There is no passage clearly referring to Christ's *literal* Coming, in which he is represented as Coming for the destruction of the Man of Sin" !—upon these two objections we shall devote yet a few pages.

The *former* part of this eighth verse, being *figurative*, then we are to interpret the *latter* part also as *figurative !* In the first place we observe that such a reason cannot be allowed to be valid, because if the *former* part of a verse, being figurative or literal, is to decide the nature of the *latter* part; then it follows that *one figurative* verse should decide the *rest of the chapter*, as being of the same-character! If Mr. Lyon then maintains his ground here, we must compel him to *Spiritualize* the *whole* of the chapter! But the gross inconsistency of maintaining this is seen, because of such being held, while the *whole* context is allowed, indisputably to refer to his *literal* Coming! The context is allowed to have reference all through to his *literal* Advent; but when the Apostle brings the subject down to the Personal Coming of Christ, for the destruction of the Apostasy, and consequently the utter annihilation of all thoughts of a *Post*millennial Advent,—why, then it is a *figurative* form of expression! When our brethren find their Theory hereby *sawn asunder*, they break through all rules of consistent exegesis to make Scripture fit and square with their system; and they bend to the stern demands of an hypothesis, rather than Scripture truth! With what consistency, indeed, they claim a *figurative* meaning here, will be seen, when it is observed that these two words παρουσια and επιφανεια are granted their *literal* meaning, every where else in Paul's Epistles! Παρουσια occurs THIRTEEN times in the Apostle's writings, and in *twelve* cases out of *thirteen* our brethren allow it to mean what it really does mean, *a literal personal Coming !* Επιφανεια occurs SIX times in the Apostle's writings, and in *five* cases out of *six*, our brethren allow to mean, what it really does mean,—*a visible manifestation!* What consistency is there here? Surely the most unfavorably disposed towards our views, will here exclaim,—how unfortunate that Mr. Lyon should be necessitated when his Theory is *at stake*, to denude these two words of their plain unsophisticated meaning, as granted them every where else in Paul's Epistles! This tells fearfully against Mr. Lyon! He is here shorn of every shade of consistency, and stands charged with yielding to a system, rather than Scripture truth, when his theory is here opposed by a declaration of his Advent in the strongest terms, and the context rendering it utterly impossible for him to escape, why then it is "a *mere passing allusion*, introduced *parenthetically, incidentally*"! We are sorry to find Mr. Lyon thus writing upon such a passage—upon such a theme,—"a *passing allusion*, introduced *parenthetically! incidentally!* No! the infallible spirit of God never wrote thus! Mr. Lyon, I am sure, could never have intended these words to have their legitimate meaning.

But let us now come a little closer to the point he holds on to as supporting his *figurative* meaning of verse 8. Because the *former* part of that verse is unmistakably *figurative*, so the *latter* part it is contended must be so to. Now as we have already said, if the figurative or literal *part* of a verse, is to decide the nature of the *rest* of that verse, *irrespective* of the context; why then *one* figurative verse must decide the nature of the *next*, and so on; and thus Mr. Lyon ought to make the *whole chapter figurative!* If again upon his principle of dealing with Mr. Rees, the meaning of this verse is to be decided, why then he ought also to make the *whole chapter figurative!* But if we are to settle the matter upon a more reasonable basis, if he allows that he erred in his dealing with Mr. Rees, as I am sure he will,—why then the only alternative appears to be for an *impartial investigation*, to decide whether two forms of expression occurring in this disputed verse, are obviously *alike*, figurative; or *one* figurative, and the *other* literal! The context, we hold decides the matter already in our favor; but we wish to convince our brethren of error upon this point, and since they will not take the context as of sufficient weight; we are willing to try the matter upon another foundation. Then are these two forms of expression *alike* figurative? Or are they *respectively* figurative and literal? With regard to the *latter part* of the verse, it must be essentially a *literal* form of expression; because Mr. Lyon and his class of interpreters allow παρουσια to be *literal* in *twelve cases* out of *thirteen*, where it occurs in Paul's Epistles: and επιφανεια they allow to be literal in *five cases* out of *six* where it occurs in Paul's Epistles; so that upon their own showing we are granted the *latter* part of verse 8, as being essentially a *literal form of expression!* What then is meant by the "Spirit of his mouth" in other portions of the Bible? Is it a *literal* form of expression? or is it a *figurative* form of expression? Here and everywhere else in Holy Writ, I believe this kind of phraseology means the preaching of the gospel, or the application of the Word of God. In Ephes. vi. 17, we read of "The sword of the Spirit," which is said to be the "Word of God"! Πνευματος is used in both cases! This then is just the same form of expression, and *cannot* in any sense be understood *literally!* Heb. iv. 12, "For the word of God is quick and powerful, and sharper than any two-edged sword." The same form of expression again, which *cannot* be understood *literally!* Rev. i. 16, "And out of his mouth went a sharp two-edged sword." Just the same form of expression again, which *cannot* allow of a *literal* acceptation! Jer. xx. 9, "His word was in my heart as a burning fire." Same form of expression again. John vi. 63, "The words that I speak unto you they are spirit and they are life"! Now in all these cases adduced, just the same kind of phraseology as in this disputed 8th verse, I dont believe there is to be found one Commentator of any class or party, that would not without a moment's hesitation declare, that they are all essentially *figurative* forms of expression, that *cannot* in any sense be understood *literally!* And we have just observed with respect to παρουσια and επιφανεια that they are according to Mr. Lyon and his class, *literal* forms of expression; *everywhere else* in Paul's Epistles used to denote a *Personal Coming of the Lord!* Then the result hereby *proved* is that Mr. Lyon stands I should think speechless upon the ground of *consistency!* He must here be charged with the crime of denuding this verse of its *legitimate* meaning! These two forms of expression occurring in this verse, we have decided as *respectively* figurative and literal; and Mr. Lyon's exposition is accordingly shown to be false, his objections groundless, and his theory is hereby cut up root and branch! We need no other passage in the Word of God to demonstrate a *Premillennial Coming* of Christ, this is of itself so powerfully antagonistic to any Millennium *preceding* the Second Advent; that we might here leave the subject as *irrefragably* and *demonstrably* proved! Mr. Lyon's objections to the plain common sense meaning of the passage, we have seen to be without the slightest foundation, and upon precisely the same principle as those in Daniel—"An impossibility shown to be possible," or a *disputed clause* of a verse allowed to mean what the language implies, if we can show *another clause* to be capable, of bearing a meaning that no man would dare to put upon it! The fact, that the *former clause* of verse 8, is *figurative*, cannot be denied, or in any sense held to be *literal*; and the fact that the *latter clause* of verse 8 is *literal*, cannot, with any consistency, be denied, or upon any reasonable grounds, held to be *figurative!* Such a position can only be maintained, at the expense of the whole context, and by putting upon this verse a meaning which would never have been, if it had not been for a Human Theory coming in the way to *demand it.*

Once more, upon this point, we observe that the entire fallacy of maintaining the *latter* part of this eighth verse as figurative, may be seen in just reviewing the grounds for rejecting such interpretation we have already gone over. What did the Apostle *introduce* in this chapter? The *literal* and personal Advent of Christ. Why did he introduce such a subject? Because his former declarations, respecting that event, had produced uneasiness in the minds of the weaker christians at Thessalonica. How did he endeavour to appease them? By telling them that such event could not take place *until* the "Mystery of iniquity," then at work, should become fully developed; and *that wicked* (lawless one, or Man of Sin) *should be revealed,* "whom the Lord should consume with the spirit of his mouth, and destroy with the brightness of his Coming"! Then it is plain that this must be his same *literal* and personal Coming, as was referred to in the *opening* of the chapter and in his former Epistle; for *herein* consists the consolation he had for these diffident believers,—the Coming, which had alarmed them, not taking place *until* "that wicked" or lawless one should be revealed, and *when* he should be revealed,—*then* the Lord should consume him with the spirit of his mouth, and destroy with the brightness of his Coming! His words, indeed, just convey something like this—Be not alarmed respecting this Coming of your Lord, for although it is true that he will come as a thief and take vengeance upon some; yet this much you may be assured of, that he *cannot* come *until* this apostasy shall be fully manifested, and this "lawless one" revealed; then, indeed, *shall it take place,* for he shall be consumed with the Spirit of his Mouth, and *destroyed* with *the brightness of his Coming.*" How such a *connected* passage, it can be attempted to show, teaches anything else, it is really surpassing strange to find; but our brethren, in so many instances, show such a determination not to accept the doctrine of a *Premillennial* coming upon *any* conditions, that we cannot after all wonder that this overwhelming and crushing passage, should meet with a similar fate.

But there is yet another shade of argument put forth by the writer of "Millennial Studies" against this part of our subject, he says (page 144) "There is no passage clearly referring to Christ's *literal* coming, in which he is represented as coming for the destruction of the man of sin"! The *validity* of such a statement will appear from our examination of his arguments on the *former* part of the eighth verse immediately preceding! But he here thinks he draws some strength from a *discrepancy* or difference in the respective accounts given of the destruction of the Apostasy, by the Prophet Daniel in his 7th chapter,— and the Apostle Paul here in Thessalonians. We are reminded that Paul's

E

account of the destruction is "*at* or *by* Christ's Coming"! while Daniel's account is "*before* his Coming"! Now it will be sufficiently obvious to every impartial student of God's Word, that such a verbal difference has no weight in it; because such destruction will be accomplished in part, doubtless, by the ministration of such means as the Son shall employ at his coming—and not solely by the might of his own arm in the extreme *literal* sense of the term. No sober mind would for a moment suppose this, consequently whether this destruction of the Apostasy be immediately at the appearance of the Son of Man, or immediately *prior* or *posterior* to it, is no reason whatever for our not accepting of such Coming in its plain *personal* and literal import! The Coming of the Son of Man and the judgments attendant thereupon, as falling upon the apostate nations, are so wrapt up in awful solemnity, so connected together, that to argue upon their *serial* order of taking place *minutely*, must be to some considerable extent *conjectural!* God nowhere deals thus minutely with events in the future, especially those events connected with his acts of judgment, being to him "strange work," and essentially his own and not man's. If the writer of "Millennial Studies" stands in need of such niceties to support his views, we would regard such views as very precarious and suspicious! But again, is it true that the "Coming of the Son of Man" is *after* the destruction of the "Man of Sin" in Daniel's account? "The Ancient of days" sits in judgment upon him, as mentioned in verses 10 and 11, then this "Coming of the Son of Man" is stated in verse 13; but because of this are we to believe that the destruction *precedes* the Coming? A few observations upon this will show the fallacy of such idea. In the first place, to *assume* such view is to do a great deal, we think; and to say the least, take up a very *bold* position: certainly, to an unitarian, such an objection, upon this point, might have, at first sight, some weight, but to those who believe in a *Triune* God, such objection dwindles down into insignificance! Who is it that is said to sit in judgment? "The Ancient of days." Then will Mr. Lyon stand by his assertion that the "Son of Man" is not *present* until *afterwards?* I know he will not. I know he cannot! Why then bring forward such objections? Why, it is quite common for both Father and Son to be described as sitting in judgment indiscriminately, and yet such descriptions are no difficulty to us whatever, we cannot say in any case that either is *absent!* "The *Father* judgeth *no man*, but hath committed all judgment unto *the Son*." John v. 22. "But ye are come unto Mount Sion....and to *God the Judge of all*....and to Jesus the mediator of the new covenant."

Heb. xii. 22—24. Upon the principle of such objections as we are considering, how can these two passages be reconciled? John says, "*The Father judgeth no man*, but hath committed *all* judgment unto *the Son*." But then Paul says "*God* is the Judge *of all*," and speaks of Jesus as Mediator *only*"! Such objections indeed as these, would carry us into endless confusion, if admitted as valid. There can be no doubt that the "man of sin" is represented both by Daniel and Paul as destroyed by the same power, and in the same way, and by the *same personage!* Indeed if there be anything here to reconcile, it *equally* tells *against* Mr. Lyon's view of a Spiritual Coming *only*! But again, is it true that this "Coming of the Son of Man" in Daniel is represented as *after* the destruction of the "man of sin"? "The Ancient of days" sits in judgment upon him, as mentioned in verses 10 and 11, and this "Coming" is mentioned in verse 13. But, if because of this "Coming" being mentioned *after* the sitting in judgment, we are to believe the "Coming" to be *posterior*,—then the *reverse* of this might be argued, because the *infliction* of this selfsame judgment is mentioned again *after* the "Coming of the Son of Man"! see verses 21 and 22. "I beheld and the same horn made war with the Saints, and prevailed against them, *until* 'the Ancient of days' came, and judgment was given to the Saints of the Most High, *and the time came* that the Saints possessed the kingdom." Here we are taught that this "horn" which was diverse from all the rest, makes war with the saints *until the time comes* that they "possess the kingdom." Now *when* do the Saints get possession of the kingdom? *Before* the Son of Man comes! They only take possession *at his coming*! consequently the *sitting* of 'the Ancient of days,' and the '*destruction*' of the Apostasy, and his '*Coming*' are *synchronous*. See verses 13 and 14. We have there a description of this "Coming of the Son of Man."—and he is represented *then* as receiving this kingdom of the Saints. So that we gather by a fair collation of Daniel's statements, precisely the *same idea* as Paul gives us—the destruction of the Apostate "Man of Sin," "*at and by* his Coming." And the result of which is, the *universal* kingdom of Messiah set up, and his *universal* reign during the Millennial era, which will lapse into the permanent state of the people of God upon earth! Mr. Lyon's arguments then hitherto, are seen upon this point as well, to be of no force!

But we are further directed to the phraseology employed in the latter part of the chapter, where it is said—"judgment was given to *the Saints* of the Most High.... the judgment shall sit, and they *(the Saints)* shall take away his dominion, to consume it unto the end." Daniel vii. 22, 26. "We who regard the Prophet and Apostle (it is added) as using *figurative* language have no difficulty in reconciling these *discrepancies*, but how can they be reconciled by Millenarians who interpret both Prophet and Apostle *literally* "? (page 145). Had the writer of these lines been kind enough to point out more clearly *where* this *discrepancy* he talks about, is to be found, why then we might have been enabled more fully to correct to our minds his mistaken notion! I do not know whether he intends that we should understand him here as believing that the judgment is committed now *entirely* to the Saints! If, however, this be the import of his reasoning, we would direct his attention to verses 9 and 10, which he quotes, but from some cause or other, *omits* a clause which just meets his argument here; if we are correct in supposing him to think the judgment is confined to the Saints, and not inflicted by either the "Ancient of days," or the "Son of Man"! We will quote these verses from him, and supply in italics the clause *omitted*, "The Ancient of days did sit ....a fiery stream came forth from before him; *thousand thousands ministered unto him, and ten thousand times ten thousand stood before him,* the judgment was set, and the books were opened." Dan. vii. 9 and 10. Now if our supposition above be correct, in Mr. Lyon's thinking the judgment in the latter part of the chapter to be confined to the Saints *alone,* and consequently show something like a discrepancy here, between the Prophet and the Apostle Paul; we have in this clause he *omitted,* a full and satisfactory solution of the error he here seems to fall into,—the "Ancient of days" sits in judgment, but as we before observed, the infliction of this judgment is effected by the *ministration* of those sainted ones about him!—they *minister* to his wishes —and this is quite accordant with other express declarations of the same event here alluded to. For example, in our notices of Zech. 14, we saw there the Lord descending, "*and all his saints with him*"! In the 19th chapter of Rev. we have the same personage seated on a "White Horse," coming down and all "*the armies in heaven following.*" And if you read at your leisure that chapter describing precisely the same events as Daniel in his 7th chapter, you will observe the striking similarity of character between the "King of Kings and Lord of Lords," mentioned by John, and the "Ancient of days" mentioned by Daniel! No reasonable man can doubt but the mysterious personage in both places, is the same as Paul speaks of as coming for the destruction of the selfsame apostasy. Where the Father is there is the Son; where the Son is there is the Father.— "I and my Father are one"! "He that hath seen me hath seen the Father.' In the 14th verse of Jude we have him described as coming with "*ten thousand* of his Saints to execute judgment"! 1 Cor. vi. 2. "Do ye not know that the *Saints shall judge the world*"? And in Matt. xiii. 41, "The Son of Man *shall send forth his angels*, and they shall gather out of his kingdom all things that offend, and them which do iniquity." So that upon this point also, we see he is equally without strength, and his objections to the *personality* of Christ's coming to destroy the "Man of Sin," are seen to be *utterly groundless!* The discrepancies so called, are no discrepancies at all, and consequently no objection. To every candid mind I should think such discrepancies now vanish, to use Mr. Lyon's own phrase, "like pillars of smoke"! It would not serve our purpose here, else we might point out many such discrepancies in the way of *his* views, although he says—" We who regard both the Prophet and the Apostle as using *figurative* language, have *no difficulty* in reconciling such discrepancies"! His *figurative*, mode of interpretation we fully admit is very *accommodating*, but still we think we could tax his ingenuity, not a little, great as it is, to put on the semblance of consistency *even* upon his principle of interpretation!

Upon the subject of '*discrepancy*' we might here ask Mr. Lyon when he recommends his readers, wishing to see a fuller discussion of the subject, to the able works of Dr. Brown, of Glasgow, and the Hon. and Rev. S. Waldegrave, M.A. How he reconciles the '*discrepancy*' between these two writers with his '*own views*'? Dr. Brown thinks we are on the *Eve of the Millennium*: Mr. Waldegrave that it is *already passed!* Dr. Brown thinks we shall soon see that *blessed era*: Mr. Waldegrave that we are *now in that ' little season' after its close*, when the Devil is *let loose again!* Dr. Brown thinks the 'good time coming,' *will soon be here*, "when the earth shall be filled with the knowledge of the Lord, as the waters cover the sea." Mr. Waldegrave that, *that time came before the Reformation, and ceased when it took place*. Dr. Brown thinks the ' little season ' will be a *bad one*: Mr. Waldegrave that it will be a *good one!* Dr. Brown thinks this earth will be *the abode of Christ and his church!* Mr. Waldegrave that such will *never be the case!* We say nothing further here, respecting these two men being the exponents of the *same views* Mr. Lyon in his recommendation of their works, professes to hold himself; but only observe the striking truthfulness of his remark,—' We who interpret both the Prophet and Apostle figuratively, *have no difficulty* in reconciling such discrepancies.' Indeed from his recommendation of these two authors, we might ask—*what can they not reconcile?* Great as is the difference between our views and those of Mr. Lyon, we hesitate not to say, that the difference between Dr. Brown and Mr.

Waldegrave is *far greater!* and yet Mr. Lyon wishes his readers to consult both, as though he could *endorse the views of either!* Mr. Lyon's power of reconciliation must be *great indeed!!*

We have already said that should the Prophet Daniel here be understood to teach us that the 'Ancient of days' sits in judgment and consumes the apostasy *before* the coming of the Son of Man,' here spoken of, it would yield Mr. Lyon no support; nor show any *real* discrepancy between the Prophet and the Apostle! 'The Ancient of days' cannot upon that view *exclude* the presence of the *Eternal Son*, co-equal with the Father! But there are many eminent and learned men, both *Pre*millenarians and *Post*millenarians, who make the Ancient of days here to refer to *the Son* in a *primary* sense! Dr. Cumming for example has the following remarks upon Rev. i. 12—16. "1 saw in the midst of the seven candlesticks, one like unto *the Son of Man*,....*his head and his hairs were white like wool*. as white as snow, and his eyes were as a flame of fire,... his feet like unto fine brass, as if they burned in a furnace,....out of his mouth went a sharp two-edged sword (the spirit of his mouth in 2 Thes. ii. 8), and his countenance was as the sun shineth in his strength." "This is the *imagery* of the *being Daniel saw*;" and thus we *identify* him who appeared to John in the Apocalypse; with *him* who appeared to Daniel in ancient prophecy—*the one Christ!* and thus *either* record is the prediction of the sufferings through which his church should pass, and the glory into which she will culminate at the last day" (page 30 Expository Readings from the Book of Revelation). The Rev. Ingram Cobbin, M.A., in his very excellent annotated Bible has the following observations upon Daniel 7, which dissipates every appearance of discrepancy that could be imagined. "The Ancient of days,"—the *Eternal Judge* of the world. Rev. xvi. 5. "Thou art righteous O Lord, which art, and wast, and shall be, because thou hast judged thus" (i.e. the Alpha and Omega, the first and the last in Rev. i. 11. and as Mr. Fuller observes,—"These are the words of *Christ*, as is manifest from Rev. i. 1, & xxii. 6-16. It was Jesus Christ and not the Father who communicated through the angel with his servant John. The Father is sometimes referred to in the Prophecy, but if I mistake not, in the third person only; not as 'speaking,' but as 'spoken of." v. 26. 'The judgment shall sit,' &c. Mr. Cobbin continues—"This being the last of the four *earthly* kingdoms or monarchies, when that is destroyed there will be *an end to the present state of things*. when all *human* rule, authority, and power, shall cease, 1 Cor. xv. 24. "Then cometh the *end*, when he shall have delivered up the kingdom to God, even the

Father, when he shall have put down all rule, and all authority, and power.' Rev. xi. 15. ' The kingdoms of this world shall become the kingdom of our Lord and of his Christ.' " (Notes on Daniel 7.)   Mr. Cobbin here then, like Dr. Cumming, makes out the 'Ancient of days,' to refer to the *Second person* in the Trinity—the *Eternal Judge* of the world, he, to whom *all* judgment hath been committed;   The setting up of this kingdom too, he makes out to be *at the end* of all *earthly* rule and power; and not apply to a mixed state of tares and wheat like Mr. Lyon.   He says that it refers to that age, that will succeed *the end* of this! when they that ' *are Christ's* ' at his *Coming*, shall have been raised; and the living *changed;* when he shall deliver up his mediatorial power to God the Father, from whom he received it,—that God may be all and in all!

Upon his view of Christ delivering up his *mediatorial* kingdom, we would differ from him, for we hold that Christ, from all eternity, *has been* Mediator, and *will*, to all eternity, be Mediator!   " He *ever liveth* to make intercession! " Mr. Lyon, we think, commits a similar mistake, when he says " Christ will continue on his throne as King though not as Priest," (page 7.) Also upon Rev. i. 12, 16, Mr. Cobbin *identifies* the Son of Man—Jesus Christ—the Second person in the Trinity, with the "Ancient of days"—in Dan. vii.—" One clothed"—the description is that of a most glorious person, clothed in robes of majesty ; see Dan. vii. 9.—*his vision,*—the metaphors here may signify as follows   (14)—" Head, *white like wool*,"—wisdom. " Eyes, &c."—omniscience. (15)—" Feet, &c."—strength, protection.   " Seven Stars,—the ministers of the churches. (20)—" Two-edged sword,"—*the Word of God*, with which he shall subdue and conquer,—Ephes. vii. 17.—2 Thess. ii. 8. ! (18)—" That liveth and was dead," —*once dead in the tomb in my human nature*, but now your ever-living *High Priest and Saviour.*" (Notes on Rev. i.)   Mr. Cobbin here makes out the " Ancient of days" to be Christ again; and thus, uniformly, in his expository notes, although not a Millenarian, does he stand in opposition to Mr. Lyon. Indeed, I think the *discrepancy* he here talks about is such that he would find some difficulty in getting many, even upon his own side, to bear him out in! The uniform testimony of Scripture is, we believe, that the destruction of the Apostasy, in its *final stage* is *at* and *by* the appearance of the Son of God.— Paul teaches this view in 2 Thess. ii. 1, 8, as we have already proved. John, in common with Paul and Daniel, teaches the same in Rev. xix. 11, 21.   The Son of Man, or King of Kings and Lord of Lords there descends upon a white horse, accompanied by the armies of heaven (Daniel's "thousand thousands ministering unto him," and Zechariah's "All his saints with him") ; and then the vast slaughter of the anti-christian confederacy follows. The stale argument about the " white horse "—"beast, &c.," being *literal*, is here to no purpose at all. We must interpret Scripture by Scripture if we wish to get *at the truth*; and not *exclude* the exercise of discrimination between letter and figure! Mr. Lyon's question—"Is Christ, at his *literal* Advent from heaven, to be sitting on a " white horse" ?—might be answered, by asking, in reply—" Did he go to the slaughter, at his first *literal* Advent, as a *literal* lamb ? If Mr. Lyon can see no difficulty in understanding such a phrase as *betokening* his *meekness* at his first *literal* Advent: why should he hesitate to accept of the " white horse," as *betokening* his *victory* at his Second *literal* Advent ? Or to take another symbolical part of prophecy, relating to his first Advent, Mr. Lyon himself uses against Mr. Rees. " Many *Bulls* have compassed me, strong *Bulls* of Bashan have beset me round, they gaped upon me with their mouths, as a ravening and a rearing Lion,"—Psalm xxii. 12, 13   Surely if Mr. Lyon finds nothing to embarrass and perplex, in employing the figure of a " *Bull*," and a " *Lion*," in association with Christ in the days of his flesh ; and *connected* with his first *literal* Advent : he need not be embarrassed and perplexed here by the figure of a " *white horse*," in association and connection with his Second *literal* Advent ! Does Mr. Lyon refuse to accept of his *literal* coming, because of the " *white horse* " being associated with that Coming ?   Upon what principle then does he associate these " Bulls," " Lions." " Lambs, &c." with his *literal* first Coming ? We might cast to the moles and to the bats the rest of his interrogations here, in a similar way.—" Is he to have upon his head many crowns" ?   " Is he to be clothed with a vesture dipped in blood " ?   " Is he to have a sharp sword proceeding out of his mouth," &c.   But we have already said sufficient upon the *strength* of such interrogations, in our remarks upon the verse—" Consume with the spirit of his mouth, and destroy with the brightness of his Coming." We therefore leave such interrogations, as needing not any further notice here. We have now not only dissipated his arguments upon his own *assumed* foundation ; but have brought forward, unquestionably, eminent men, on both sides of the controversy, denying his *very foundation*, and upsetting the only grounds upon which he attempted to draw forth this argument against the *visible* appearance of the Son !

We might, I think, now leave 2 Thess. ii. 1, 8, as clearly destructive to Postmillennialism, both root and branch ; and as *demonstrably* teaching that the

Mr. LYON'S ARGUMENT from PAUL KNOWING the 'TIMES & the SEASONS.' 37

Second Coming of Christ will be for the destruction of the 'Man of Sin, as well as to *introduce* the Millennium! There is, however, another shade of argument the writer of "Millennial Studies" has derived, he thinks, from this chapter, telling against the argument of Millenarians, "That the Millennium *intervening* between the present time and the Advent of our Lord, destroys the possibility of watchfulness, enjoined by so many passages of Scripture." He allows that Christians are represented therein as 'looking,'—'waiting,'—and 'watching' for his Advent, called the "blessed hope." He admits that such passages as the following all refer to his *personal* Coming.—"Surely I come quickly," "Behold he cometh with clouds," &c. These he says, and many more similar portions of Scripture, we fully admit refer to the time when "He shall come in the glory of the Father, with all the holy angels." "Moreover we freely acknowledge that the return of the Saviour is held forth as the 'blessed hope' of the church, and as the *grand epoch around which the desire and expectation of Christians should constantly be gathering*; there has certainly been a *tendency to overlook this* among Christians.   In their conceptions of heaven, they have been apt to dwell rather on the blessedness of the *intermediate state* of being 'absent from the body and present with the Lord,' *than on the blessedness* in reserve for the believer *on the revelation of Christ from heaven*.   We think that *Millenarians have rendered an important service to the church, by directing attention to the prominence which the inspired writings give to the Second Advent*"! Now really we cannot help here congratulating Mr. Lyon upon being far, very far in advance of many of his brethren in his views of the Second Advent.   We rejoice to see him thus speak out, and declare the importance of looking for that "blessed hope." We rejoice that he is persuaded that his brethren by their Millenarianism have 'rendered an *important service to the church*,' because he virtually here admits both the *good resulting from it*, and also that the Second Advent is the *proper object* of the Christian's hope! We think there is a marked difference in some of Mr. Lyon's views bearing upon the subject, to what other writers before him have manifested; his views of the 'new heaven and new earth,' forming the abode of the redeemed family of God; the great concession virtually made in the above extract *in our favor*, his views of the Millennium altogether, declare that his tone of theology is quite altered from many writers before him on the same side; in fact, he is a very good Millenarian, but unfortunately mistaken as to the *time* of the Second Advent.   I feel persuaded that if Dr. Cumming and the Messrs. Birks and Bonar were to wait upon him, as a deputation, and entreat him to be

F

decided, he would at once forego his only hindrance—that of *cutting away* from all those passages, the *personal* Advent of Christ to *introduce* the Millennium; and become a Millenarian! He would make a first class man should he join our ranks and take up the '*better side*' of the argument to defend. But what shall we say after all this, when he attempts to set aside the fact, that Paul intended to convey the idea, that the day of Christ's Coming, *might* overtake the Thessalonians as a thief; and draw forth from this, an argument to justify himself, in being placed with his own views in such a position, that obedience to his Lord's injunctions, " to watch," *is to him a thing impossible!*

Mr. Lyon says " we need *not* enquire to what extent it was given to Paul to know ' the times and the seasons'; this much he evidently *did* know, that the day of Christ's Coming, was yet in the *far distant* future. (page 94.) Then he goes on to say, "We cannot feel there is any force in the question asked by Millenarians—' How can we look out for the Saviour's Coming, if we believe that a thousand years are to *intervene* before it ?'" To this he says it is sufficient to reply—"How did the inspired writers look for it ? Though they *knew* that events must previously occur, which would necessarily occupy lengthened periods of time; and which have actually filled up thousands of years"! (page 97.) From all this, the strange conclusion he comes to is, that " Christ put his followers in possession of such knowledge regarding the future, that obedience to his injunctions, *was to them a thing impossible?* Now surely this is a strange *finale* to come to, upon a subject so important! A conclusion Mr. Lyon should only have arrived at, when his grounds for such reasoning had been found sufficient to justify him; *then* only should he have added—"the Bible is a book, according to Millenarians, the more closely it is studied, the less possible is it to live in harmony with its precepts"!

The fact is this, Mr. Lyon's foundation here is built upon sand; he is reasoning upon an entirely *assumed* basis! "We need *not* enquire," he says, "to what extent it was given the Apostle Paul to know the times and the seasons; this much he evidently *did* know, that the day of Christ's Coming was yet in the far *distant* future." Now we say here, upon a subject so vastly important in its results, Mr. Lyon should ' *have* enquired,' instead of excusing himself by saying ' We need *not* enquire'! He should have ' *investigated*' the grounds upon which he here reasons, instead of taking ' *for granted*,' his foundation, which of course, if false, upsets the whole of his reasoning, and certainly leaves him in such a position with his own views, that obedience to his Lord's injunctions,—" to watch," *is to him a thing impossible '*

In the first place we ' *will* enquire ' to what extent the Apostle was probably favored with information, respecting ' the times and seasons ' ; and in doing so we shall just advert to Daniel and John, who both treat of this self-same apostasy, and see if we can gather anything from them, in warranting us to conclude that Paul *knew* so much respecting " the times and seasons " as to be *certain* that the day of Christ's Coming was in the *far distant* future ! Daniel then, far more experienced in visions and revelations of the Lord than ever Paul was, was not permitted to know " the times and the seasons." In his vision of the fourth beast there is contained this self-same Man of Sin alluded to by Paul here in his Epistle to the Thessalonians, and the self-same Man of Sin alluded to by John in his Apocalypse ; and yet Daniel was not favored with any knowledge respecting ' the times and the seasons ;' nay even afterwards when he *requested* this very information, which Mr. Lyon assumes Paul had—*he got it not* ! Daniel saw two angelic beings on either side of the bank of the river,—" and one said to the man clothed in linen, ' How long shall it be to the end of these wonders" ? The man clothed in linen, sware that it would be, " for a time, and times, and the dividing of time." Was Daniel then put in possession of the ' *How long* '? Hear him, " I heard, but I *understood not* " ! Then he asks again, " O my Lord what shall be the end of these things ?" The answer is—" Go thy way Daniel, for the words are *closed up* and *sealed* till the time of the end " ! Go thy way *till* the end be, for thou shalt rest and stand in thy lot at the end of the days. It is enough for you Daniel to be assured that when, those " many *from among* them that sleep in the dust of the earth shall awake," you shall be found among them in your proper place—go and rest—" it is not for you *to know* ' the times or the seasons,' which the Father hath put *in his own power* " !

Daniel then we find, was not favored with any knowledge respecting ' the times and the seasons.' Let us see if we can gather anything to the contrary from John. In his Apocalyptic vision he has the great drama of the earth laid open to his view, from his own time down to the period of the final judgment ; but did he get at ' the times and the seasons ' ? Dates to be sure are introduced here and there, but like Daniel's ' time, and times, and the dividing of time,' they were wrapped up in enigmatical numbers ! Like Daniel he has an angelic interpreter to unfold the vision of the beast, but *no information* is given respecting the time *of its duration* ! What then is the conclusion to be come to here upon the subject ? We have seen that Daniel did *not* know ' the times and the seasons ' with respect to *this* apostasy. John evidently did *not* know ' the times and the seasons' with respect to this selfsame apostasy.   Where then, we ask, is the evidence to justify Mr. Lyon in *assuming*, that Paul knew what Daniel and John did not ?   When the disciples asked our Lord if he would *then* restore the kingdom to Israel— did he inform them of 'the times and the seasons'? The answer was—"*it is not for you to know* 'the times or the seasons,' which the Father hath put *in his own power*"!   Where then, we ask again, is the evidence for *assuming* that Paul knew *more* than his fellow disciples ?   Was it communicated to him in visions ?   Where then is it recorded ?   In what chapter and verse is such information to be found ?   Mr. Lyon's base here is seen to be *false*, and the whole of his superstructure consequently useless,—' the times and the seasons' were not communicated to either the Prophet or any of the Apostles—being kept secret with the Father ! Mr. Lyon then is here seen to be without *precedent* in apostolic times, and we think, placed in such a position, that obedience to his Lord's injunctions ' to watch,' *is to him a thing impossible !*

But again, we think it would not be sufficient to meet the demands of Post-millennialism here, to suppose that Paul knew, what none of his fellow Apostles or the Prophet Daniel did know.   If Paul had this information, we still think the supposition would be inadequate to the demands here made upon it.   It would still be insufficient to justify our brethren in placing themselves in such a position, as we would fancy the *inspired* Apostle to be ! If such injunctions as we are speaking of, were unnecessary to Paul; that would be no reason for supposing they were at all unnecessary to us. If Paul's information were such, that he need not be told ' to watch ' *always*,—in other words, if he saw the end from the beginning—if he could penetrate by his *inspiration* the vista of futurity, and thus be enabled to satisfy himself that Christ could not come in his day,—that would not be sufficient to justify us in regarding ourselves as placed in an *analagous position!* Mr. Lyon to gather any support here, must be capable of shewing not only that the Apostle *had* this information , but also that he deemed it prudent for others to have the same, by making it *known to them*, and this too, in such a manner, that any believer in Christ can also make himself acquainted with such information ! Supposing the Apostle to have known that thousands of years were to intervene between his time, and the period of such Advent, where did he inform his brethren of such fact ?   In what Epistle is such an idea to be gathered ?   We say, such information to meet the demands of Mr. Lyon here, must be to be found in the Apostle's writings, else we are led inevitably as without it, to the conclusion that he is without a shadow of ground to justify himself, in looking yet for a thousand years to intervene between the present and that day; and thus placing himself in such a position, that the possibility of 'watchfulness,' *is to him a thing impossible!* We repeat the question, in what Epistle, chapter and verse, is such information to be got ? We reply to the silent negative answer—No, indeed, such teaching is not to be found in the writings of the Apostle. In no place can such an idea be gathered—and in no sense can such a liberty or dispensation from 'watching' be justified from his teaching. What indeed would become of the many exhortations ' to watch' for his Advent as taking place at *any* time, suddenly, and unknown to *any* man. They must inevitably become, upon such a supposition, unnecessary, if not indeed, delusive ! What would become of the *honesty* of the Apostle in exhorting them to be circumspect and moderate in everything, *because* " the Lord was *at hand*" ? What would become of the *truthfulness* of the Apostle in telling the Thessalonians that " the day of the Lord so cometh as a thief in the night—that when men should say peace and safety, then sudden destruction cometh upon them, (and because of this) *therefore* let *us* not sleep, but *watch* and be sober " ? Did the Apostle only mean to *frighten* them into watchfulness,—if so, we could, perhaps, admire the *end*, but not the means *employed ;* we would praise the motive, but at the same time believe such means to be quite contrary, both to the Apostle's persuasive manner, and also the genius of the Gospel ! No. we cannot allow that he here, or in any other case, put before them the duty of ' watching' for his Coming ; and at the same time either knowing or believing that such would not take place for thousands of years to come ! The Apostle did *not* know the ' times and the seasons ' which the Father hath put in his own power, we feel assurred (and supposing he had *known*) he did *not* convey such information to his brethren, this is quite certain, he says ' ye have *no need* that I write unto you respecting ' the times and the seasons,' for yourselves *know,* perfectly, "that the day of the Lord so cometh as a thief in the night." Then it is quite plain he did *not* communicate such information, if he had it ; but says, ye have ' *no need,*' of such information,—this much you *do know* perfectly, that he will come suddenly ' even as a thief in the night,' and knowing *this much,* ' ye are not in darkness ' that it should overtake you as a thief,—not watching for such an event, nay, *this* very information respecting its suddenness, being made known to you—" Ye are thereby made ' children of the day,' not of the night nor of darkness, in this particular, *therefore* let *us* not sleep on this account, but ' *watch*' and be sober ! let *us* not be seen as children of the night, but of the day,—not '*sleeping*' when we should be '*watching*' ! In his Second Epistle no more information is given than that 'the mystery of iniquity,' then at work, should first become fully developed, and then the object of watching should be turned into welcome; instead of conveying the idea of a lengthened period of time *intervening*, he seems rather to have led them to suppose that such should be looked upon as *brief*, and at the most, *uncertain!* Indeed, how can we suppose the Apostle would here so soon contradict his teaching in his former letter,—did he *make a mistake* in his first Epistle? Where does he acknowledge such a thing? The 'mystery of iniquity' *then* worked, its consummation being, as to time, *a secret*, and beyond the perception of man to tell even when it should become ripe for destruction and the Advent, being to be characterized by suddenness, the many injunctions to be '*always ready*,' ever found 'watching,' led the Apostle to teach his followers to look for such event, as occurring at *any* time; the statement that such might be 'at even, or at midnight, or at the cock crowing, or in the morning,' was made to the Apostles in order that they should 'ever watch,' and consequently binding upon those at Thessalonica, as well as their successors in all ages —"Watch ye, therefore, for ye know not the day nor the hour (the times or the seasons) when your Lord shall come." "What I say unto *you* I say unto *all*.—Watch"! Although the Apostle then checked the unhappy tendency of his first Epistle, in this particular, by telling them of the *prior* consummation of the Apostasy; he by no means led them to suppose that 'watchfulness,' on their part, was *less* a duty,—on the contrary,—exhorted them to bear in mind the same great event, and so "patiently wait for Christ" this he certainly could not have done with any consistency, if, as Mr. Lyon assumes, he knew such would not be for a *lengthened* period of time, or that the day of his coming was in the *far distant* future! he is, consequently, shorn of every shade of defence whereby to screen himself in *now* looking for an intervention of a thousand years, and so putting himself in such a position, that obedience 'to watch' for such event, *is to him a thing impossible!*

It is a very poor apology indeed here to remind us of the fact, that Millenarians are looking themselves for events yet to transpire before his appearing; it is a very poor palliation or means of justification, to tell us there is no difference *in principle* between expecting *a few years*, and a *whole Millennium* to intervene! If the principle could be shown to be the same, surely the tendency or *practical effect* cannot be the same! Mr. Lyon or any Antimillenarian believing that a thousand years will yet transpire before the Second Advent, we are quite sure are thereby rendered incapable of obeying those injunctions ' to watch;' this must without any demur be to them, *a thing impossible!* But with any Millenarian expecting events yet to transpire, which *may* occupy in the ordinary course of things, say ten or twenty years, can it be said that his case is at all *analagous?* Is obedience to his Lord's injunctions *thereby* rendered a thing impossible to him ? If the principle can be said to be the same, can the effect be deemed at all *analagous?* Let Mr. Lyon judge of the similarity by the practical tendency, and then tell us whether there be no difference! But supposing events expected to transpire with the Millenarian, to be such as might ordinarily fill half a century, is the case then at all *analagous?* The Antimillenarian expecting a *whole* Millenary—is placed in such a position that obedience is *impossible,* not only because of the length of time exceeding by far that of his own possible earthly existence, but also because a Millenary is a *definite* period, a *real* fact, an absolute *certainty!* The Millenarian's half century is at the best only an *uncertainty,* a mere *conjecture,* and must at any rate be *precarious!* Is there no difference here in point of practical tendency, in the real facts of the two cases? Can they be said in any sense to be at all *analagous?* Will Mr. Lyon here step forward and tell us there is no difference? Will he tell us a *certainty* produces the same effect as an *uncertainty?* Will he contend for no difference between a thing *impossible,* and that which to say the least, is *highly probable?* Now this is upon the supposition that events yet to transpire *might* in the ordinary course of things occupy a period of years. but does God perform his providential rounds according to the calculations of man ? Are we to calculate in spite of his many warnings to be '*always ready,*' upon such events yet to take place, as occupying *any* number of years, when we know that the providential judgments immediately preceding and attendant upon the Second Advent, so far as their serial order of taking place is concerned, are wrapped up in almost *impenetrable* darkness? Why, for aught any man can tell, the Almighty might, as Dr. Cumming justly remarks, crowd into a few month or years, what would otherwise fill centuries he created the world in six days—he can *finish* it in infinitely less space of time, and we say, that obedience to ' ever watch,' comes in before any speculative events, and renders on the part of the Millenarian ' watchfulness' *imperative*—while it is to the Antimillenarian, *yet a thing impossible!*

Mr. Lyon's interposition here—that we are not to calculate upon miracles, is false—no miracle would be hereby performed! God has crowded events one upon another often in his providence. And rather than not being justified in expecting such to be the case with events yet future, in the Millenarian creed, we say, we have a decided indication on the part of God, that such will be so! In the 24th of Matthew we read, that "For the Elect's sake, those days shall be *shortened*"! Now we think it is manifestly obvious that the events here alluded to, cannot have reference to the destruction of Jerusalem, this *unparalleled* desolation cannot yet be passed; because we are informed the time preceding the Second Advent, will be *unprecedented*, and the judgments *unparalleled*! Our Lord then, it would seem, in speaking of the Jewish catastrophe here, sweeps along to the still greater which awaits the Gentile; the Jewish being in some sense a type of the latter, he took occasion to speak from the type of that which was typified. "Except those should be shortened, there should no flesh be saved, but for the Elect's sake, those days shall be *shortened*"! Events then yet future instead of destroying the ground of 'watchfulness' with the Millenarian, only serve to *deepen* them, while on the contrary, the Antimillenarian as before, is still left in such a position, that obedience 'to watch,' *is to him a thing impossible*! But further, it is the belief of many Millenarians of note, that some considerable space of time will elapse between the appearing of Christ in the clouds, his risen and changed Saints joining him. and the period when he will descend to the earth! consequently many of those events, yet looked for, may take place between his appearing and his descent to the earth! The assumed or pretended *analogy* then, is left without a rag of resemblance, or the slightest shade of identification! Whatever prophecy may lead us to expect, it cannot in any sense invalidate our reasons for 'watchfulness.' Nay we would be thankful for the star-light of prophecy, but we would even forego that altogether, rather than it should suppress the rising and expecting beams of a brighter light—even the Sun of Righteousness! We are indeed glad of the help given us in Prophecy, but since man may be mistaken in his apprehension of that, we would not for one moment consent to its destroying, or suppressing in any degree, the incontrovertible evidence we have of the fact, that the day of Christ's coming, must ever be regarded as "*at hand*"! We *may* indeed be mistaken in our views of Prophecy,—but we ought not to have any hesitation in accepting of such declarations as appropriate and intended for *us*. "Take heed to yourselves, lest at any time your hearts be overcharged with surfeiting and drunkenness, and cares of this life, an so *that day* come upon you *unawares*, for as a snare shall it come upon all them that dwell upon the face of the whole earth,—"*watch ye therefore and pray always.*" "What I say unto *you*, I say unto *all*, watch"!

Mr. Lyon's reasoning upon Mr. Bickersteth's writing, as expressed in this sentence, "Our ignorance of the time of Christ's Coming, and the suddenness of it, make it impossible that there should be an intervening *certain* period of one thousand years yet to come," (vol. 8., p. 60.) is exceedingly futile. It may be said to be a reply—but certainly without invalidating, in one jot, the force of Mr. Bickersteth's remark. Mr. Lyon meets it by observing that almost *two* Millenaries have *now* elapsed since the utterance of such commands 'to watch' by Christ and his Apostles! And is this showing Mr. Bickersteth to have written *incautiously?* This Millenarian argument has nothing to do with the *possibility* of Millenaries elapsing *prior* to such Advent; but with *our foreknowledge* of such Millenaries to be clear and decided! Mr Bickersteth never meant that a thousand years *might* not yet elapse before the Coming of Christ, but that we could not, on any *possible* grounds, be justified in ho'ding '*that definite millenary*' spoken of in Rev. 20, as taking place before Christ's Coming; because such would entirely nullify every exhortation to be found in Scripture, made in order that we should '*ever* watch,' for that *unknown* and *uncertain* event! The argument of Mr. Bickersteth is that '*the* Millennium' taking place *prior* to his Coming, and not '*a* Millennium,' is a thing *impossible*, because of our duty 'to watch' for his Advent, as occurring at any time; it has nothing whatever to do with the ordinary course of time that *may* yet elapse before such Advent! Had this argument therefore been penned, as Mr. Lyon observes "*prior* to the year (A D.) 800, the result would *not have falsified his assertion*"!! How could Mr. Lyon write so recklessly upon such a plain observation? If Christ's Coming should not take place yet for a thousand years, twice told, it will *not falsify* Mr. Bickersteth's assertion!!

To maintain indeed that the Apostle's did not mean to teach us 'to watch' for the Second Coming of Christ as chronologically near, does furnish us with a novel idea of the meaning of words! With what consistency it is held, that phrases can have the signification 'to watch' for an event, and yet *not* refer to something which *may* take place in the lifetime of such as are called upon 'to watch,' we are at a loss to conceive! In maintaining such a position, it is only required to show its fallacy—to quote a passage or two here to the point,—

G

"Watch ye therefore; for ye know not when the master of the house cometh, at even or at midnight, or at cockcrowing, or in the morning· lest coming suddenly, he find *you* sleeping." Our Lord after stating that he should take a journey into a far country and *return* ; gives the above exhortation ' to watch ' for that period. Did he mean *them* ' to watch ' in the faith of that event taking place some thousands of years hence ? What then meaneth ' watch *ye*,' therefore —*ye* know not—lest he find *you* sleeping ? It would indeed be a marvellous commentary upon such a passage, that would make him out to mean, ' watching ' for such event *three thousand years after* ! Again, " Be *ye* therefore *ready*, for the Son of Man cometh at an hour when *ye* think not." Could he here mean, Be *ye* ready for my coming *three thousand years hence* ! But Mr. Lyon says there are ' *good grounds* ' for believing this passage to refer to death; however he has not told us what these ' *good grounds* ' are; else we might, perhaps, have *transferred* such ' *good grounds* ' to every other kindred passage ; and so cut away from Mr. Lyon any ' *good grounds* ' for maintaining that Christ will ever come a second time at all ! His objection really made upon this passage, is almost too futile to merit refutation. He says if it refer to the Second advent, then those ' absent from the body, and present with the Lord,' *ought* also to be *waiting* for his coming ! This, we are informed, would be absurd. Christ cannot mean in this exhortation that departed saints—should have their " loins girded about, and their lights burning, and to be like men who wait for their Lord." (page 100.) I ask Mr. Lyon if he really believes that at death the doom of man is irrevocably sealed ? Does he allow that ' as the tree falleth there it shall be ' ? Will he concede that, the soldier's warfare is ended, when he lays down his mortality ? These, we are assured, he must believe ; what then does he mean here by carrying this exhortation *beyond the grave* ? Will he carry the promises of pardon *also beyond the grave* ? What need here to enter the invisible world ? If exhortations can be carried there, surely ' offers of mercy ' may be too ! If it could be imagined necessary to ' exhort ' those ' *who rest from their labours* '; surely we might also deem it reasonable to suppose that ' entreaties ' to accept of the offers of mercy, would not be out of place to those, who like a troubled sea, in that world, " *cannot rest* " " We marvel at such argument. Can this be *one* of the ' *good grounds* ' for believing this passage to have reference to death and not to the Second Advent ? Mr. Lyon is seen here to be singularly unhappy and false in his reasoning—indeed, all through we may now fairly conclude that he is wrong and mistaken upon every point where he has attempted to scale 'Millenarian strongholds' drawn from Scripture, and particularly those passsages we have gone over. Upon Daniel vii, he was seen to be altogether out of place, and quite beside the mark in his reasoning; and upon this famous passage, in Thessalonians, which we must now take our leave of, we have likewise seen him to be just as far away from the demonstrated teaching of the Apostle, so that we may now say he is entirely mistaken in his views of the Second Advent, which is the key-stone to the whole arch, and which decides the whole controversy in our favor! We showed, in the first place, what the Apostle did intend to convey,—the idea of Christ's Coming *at* the destruction of the Apostasy, and consequent *opening* of the Millennium. We have seen Mr. Lyon's views and objections against such teaching to be fallacious upon every point,—his reasoning upon the 8th verse has been *exploded*,—his arguments, drawn from Paul, knowing 'the times and the seasons,' we have seen also to be *unfounded*,—his pretended *analogy* between Millenarian and Antimillenarian views, as alike destructive to watchfulness, *unsupported*, and we think we may now leave this passage for the present as clearly *demonstrating* *Pre*millennialism; and at the same time as clearly destroying *Post*millennialism base and fabric !

We might indeed go on with Scripture quotations teaching the same great truths, for which we have been contending, for we have no lack of support from the Sacred Oracles; but our present intention is not so much to show what *can* be said in our favor, as to prove that Mr. Lyon is wrong in the passages he has chosen, and we believe in great error upon the subject of the Second Advent. —We have, we think, said sufficient already to convince any impartial student of God's Word, that the Second Coming of Christ will be to *introduce* the Millennium ! but we will advert briefly to another portion of Scripture, from the teaching of Christ himself, that is alike fatal to the opposite view of a *Post*millennial Coming. See Matthew 13, containing the parable of the ' wheat and the tares.' When the disciples perceived that there were tares among the wheat,—wicked men mixed up with the good.—thinking like many of our brethren in modern times, that they would bring about a Millennium of man's own making—asked permission to gather out the tares from among the wheat. Now, did Christ say nay—the time has not yet come, the *fulness* of the Gentiles must first be come in, my brethren in the flesh first converted ? Not a word about any such state of things ever characterizing the present age,—the reply was, " Let both grow together until the harvest."—" The harvest is the end of the world," or this dispensation. Here then we are again informed this mixture of good and bad runs on without *any* happy Millenary to break the motly chain; the good and the bad continue 'growing together' until the end, when the Master himself shall come to separate them. Indeed our Lord's teaching here seems to be irreconcilable with Mr. Lyon's own view of that happy era, yet awaiting the world. It has generally been the custom of our brethren to *bring down* the standard of that 'good time coming' somewhat; and *to raise* the condition of this mixture a little; and thus appear to make extremes in some sense meet; but with Mr. Lyon's views, this does seem to be quite an impossibility, although we consider his view very far *below* the Scriptural standard. We will quote a few of his leading remarks upon the Millennium, which will show a discrepancy vast enough between such views and Christ's teaching here. "The Millennium will be preceded by the binding of Satan,—he will be under some kind of restraint, so that he will *cease to deceive the nations* .... the spirit will then be poured out from on high; then shall the wilderness be a *fruitful field*, only *until* then shall thorns and briers come up,—an era when religious knowledge shall be *universally* diffused, 'the earth filled with the knowledge of the Lord as the waters cover the sea.' 'The glory of the Lord revealed, and all flesh see it together.' An era of just government—the Messiah 'shall judge the people with righteousness, and the poor with equity.' 'The saints shall possess the kingdom.' 'The *greatness* of the kingdom *under the whole heaven* shall be given to the people of the saints of the Most High." Such are a few of his sentiments respecting the Millennium, and we may add, that such a view it is obvious, is quite inconsistent with the 'wheat and the tares' growing *together* right on through it! 'Satan will *cease* to deceive the nations.' Now what are the tares?—The children of the wicked one. Who sows the tares?—the Devil. Such is Christ's testimony. Then the Devil a thousand years *prior* to Christ's Coming, will *cease* to deceive the nations, he will *cease* to sow tares; and the wilderness mixture as a consequence, will become a fruitful field, but how, unless Christ's testimony here be *invalidated?* Can he *cease* to deceive the nations and the wilderness as a consequence, become a fruitful field; and yet this teaching of Christ hold good—that both the wheat and the tares *grow on together* right through the Millennium? If the Devil *cease* to sow tares, the tares must *run out* long before the Millennium, unless Mr. Lyon can demonstrate that the crop sown immediately *before* the opening of that era, will not become exhausted for a thousand years! This would be marvellous in our eyes, however easy it may seem to our brethren! Mr. Lyon talks about Millenarians calculating upon miracles, I think this surely would be a prolific and *miraculous* crop! He is here then diametrically opposed to Christ, who teaches us to believe that the Devil will keep on sowing—and consequently have without cessation a crop of tares until the Master himself comes at the harvest! Again, "an era when religious knowledge shall be *universally* diffused, 'the earth *filled* with the knowledge of the Lord, &c.' 'The glory of the Lord revealed, and *all* flesh see it together.' Religious knowledge diffused *universally*. Will the *tares* then become *saturated* with religion? The earth *filled* with the knowledge of the Lord—will the *tares* be *filled* with this knowledge? If so, why then, we ask, what will be the practical use of this, if 'the children of the wicked one' still remain wicked? 'The glory of the Lord revealed, and all flesh see it together.' The glory of the Lord is *now* revealed in some sense, in what other sense can *all* flesh see it then together? Will the 'wheat' behold this glory with *rejoicing;* and the tares with *dismay?* "An era of just government—'the saints shall possess the kingdom,' 'the *greatness* of the kingdom *under the whole heaven*, shall be given to the people of the saints of the Most High." 'An era of just government.' What are we to understand by this? The Messiah shall *then* judge the people with righteousness, &c. Does he *now* then not exercise *righteous* judgment in the earth? What means all Mr. Lyon's laboured demonstration I wonder, to show that he became invested with *universal* sovereignty, when he ascended up on high and led captivity captive? What mean the arguments to show that he *now* has 'David's throne,' and is *now* possessed of '*all* power'? Are we to understand that he *now* has '*all* power,' but does not exercise justice? Are we to understand that he *now* possesses the throne of the '*whole world*,' but will not favor us with '*just* government,' until the Millennial era? Will Mr. Lyon here contend for his '*all* power'—'*universal* sovereignty,'—'throne of the *whole* world'; and yet tell us *only* at some future time will he dispense justice in the earth,—'judge the people with righteousness, and the poor with equity'? I think Mr. Lyon is here seen to be in a kind of dilemma, he must either forego his claims to '*universal* sovereignty,' and occupation of the '*whole* world'; or he must believe that this '*just* government' of the *universal* sovereign' is *already* established; and consequently its Millennial traits now in existence! Will he here then tell us the Devil has *now* no authority! that he has *already* ceased to deceive the nations? Again, 'the saints shall possess the kingdom,' 'the *greatness* of the kingdom, *under the whole heaven*,' &c. This quotation we have before noticed in our remarks on Daniel 7, and already proved to refer to a time *after* the Second Advent. But 'the saints here, are said to possess the *greatness* of the kingdom *under the whole heaven*,' and this it is contended *precedes* the Second Advent, then the testimony of Christ demonstrates that among the saints shall *sinners* also be found, with the wheat are also the *tares* growing! therefore this *universal* kingdom of Messiah which Daniel saw in vision, must comprehend also this kingdom of Satan! The *universal* here according to Mr. Lyon, must comprehend *every part* of the same; and in Daniel's *universal* kingdom of *all* servants, *all* loyal subjects; there are 'the children of the wicked one'—*the subjects of the enemy*! Mr. Lyon then must according to his reasoning on 'David's throne' believe, that Christ will have a *universality* of dominion, all *loyal* subjects,—'*all* people, nations, and languages *serving* him'; and yet according to our Lord's declaration, 'the children of the wicked one,' the property of the enemy, will be comprehended in that *universal* possession! Mr. Lyon will have Daniel's *universal* kingdom of righteousness a thousand years *prior* to Christ's Advent:—then he *must* have in the midst of that kingdom, according to our Lord himself, all the elements of wickedness, for the Devil is there, and his subjects growing (flourishing) just as do the saints! Mr. Lyon then has here a task, we think, set before him, which his logical powers will never enable him to perform, that of showing how 'Christ can be said to have a *universality* of dominion, in the Prophecy of Daniel, '*all* people, nations, and languages, *serving him;* and also according to Christ himself—have the children of the wicked,' therewith *commingled!* We are bound then to add, that upon the Postmillennial principle the Bible is a book of confusion, speaking one thing in one place, and a contradictory thing in another place, and that notwithstanding the amputations and surgical treatment it is put to, we are still landed upon a bed of *sickness*, as well as *health; mortification* in one part, as well as *soundness* in another; and we are asked to believe whatever Mr. Lyon may say to exonerate himself, in a mere 'spectral appearance' of that bright and blessed era for which the whole creation has now been groaning six thousand years!

Finally, upon the subject of Christ's Coming being *after* the Millennium, we observe that the fallacy of such idea, to our mind, cannot be seen in a stronger light, than by comparing it with the *insuperable* mass of evidence we have of the state of the world at the Saviour's Coming. "As it was in the days of Noah—as it was in the days of Lot—even thus shall it be when the Son of Man is revealed." "There shall be mockers in the last times." "In the last days perilous times

shall come, men having a *form* of godliness, but denying the power thereof."
"When the Son of Man Cometh shall he find faith on the earth," &c., &c.
Indeed, the means resorted to in order to reconcile such statements with a Postmillennial Coming have been truly sad,—the Millennium brought down to a
mere spectre!—the blessings attendant thereupon, *circumscribed!*—the binding of
Satan made *merely nominal!*—the Book of Revelations treated almost as if *not
canonical*—deemed almost *suspicious*—merely symbolical, and to be received
with caution—not allowed to have that meaning attached to its forms of
expression any other Book would! We would not indeed charge Mr. Lyon
with all this,—he has not gone to the same length as Mr. Brown, and many
before him: we fully admit there are concessions made in his work that we
are pleased to see; but still we are compelled to add there is much in it we are
grieved to find, and which we feel bound to reject, as clearly unscriptural and
mistaken. "It is a mistake, (we are told,) to regard the Millennium as an era
when men will be *universally* converted to God." "Thy people shall be *all
righteous*," Isaiah lx. 21. "They shall not teach every man his neighbour, and
every man his brother, saying, Know the Lord. for *all* shall know me, *from the
least to the greatest*," Heb. viii. 11. Such passages as these teach not that *all* will
be righteous, it is contended! "It is not (says Mr. Lyon) for us to say what
proportion of the world's population will be truly Christian, during the Millennium: the predicted revolt, at its close, shows vast numbers will have been
but Christians in name," (page 71.) Such is his *spectral* view of that era! But
with all due respect to him, we beg to state that such revolt, predicted, shows
nothing of the kind!—the revolt alluded to is the result of Satan's liberation
after the Millennium! It shows no such thing, while Satan is bound, as that
vast numbers will have been but Christian *in name*! If such passages as these
in Isaiah and Hebrews, and many other predictions to the same import, are to
be thus marred, and made to have reference *only* to the church in the sense our
brethren regard them; why, then according to the idea of no *personal* Coming
at the *opening* of the Millennium, and only a nominal binding of Satan, *we may
now be in the midst of that happy era!!'* We may expect nothing probably better
than *at present!* Nay, if such passages may be said to apply to the church,
while there are also *worldly men*, why the numbers of the church may be *vastly
smaller* than *now*!! They may not be at all to be compared with the present
state of Christendom, for "thy people shall be *all* righteous," may apply to the
church in such a case,—her numbers being, *however, small!!* If this be not

narrowing the Millennium to a '*shadow or a spectre*,' I know not what can! In fact, I gladly quote here a few sentences from another *Post*millennial writer who entirely *denies* one half of Mr. Lyon's reasoning, and fully allows of the truthfulness of these remarks.   The Rev. R. W. M'c All, of Sunderland, in a reply to a Pamphlet of Mr. Rees' already alluded to, has the following observations.—"Though not a *Pre*millennialist, I stand before you '*a watcher*' for the *Second* Advent of my Lord, and I regard it, as my duty, *each day and hour*, to '*wait for*' his appearing! We may estimate and study and strain all our little ingenuity, yet be *utterly wrong* in every one of our calculations respecting the consummation.   Has he not said that when he comes to judgment that '*day*' shall arrive '*as a thief in the night!*   Whenever he appears it will be just when none could have calculated upon his Advent.   Hence, though privileged, to come to Prophecy, 'as a light that shineth in a dark place,' and though that light seems to tell us that the end is not yet, we may be completely *in error*, and Premillennialists too!   The thief may arrive *in an hour*—in a *moment!* so as I lay my head upon my pillow this very night, I would desire to hold myself *in a waiting posture*, lest, ere the morning dawn, the Judge should *be here*"! page 21.   Here, this writer falls in with our sentiments entirely, respecting his *thief-like* Advent, and quite shuns the daring liberty taken by those who look yet, for a *defined* Millenary!   But we will quote a few more lines from Mr. M'c All, where he *denies* the whole of Mr. Lyon's reasoning upon Paul *knowing* the Times and the Seasons, and expresses himself as though we might *already* be *at the close of that happy period!*   "All our calculations concerning coming events may be *erroneous*!   The Millennium *may now be closing instead of commencing*! (What a pity this writer, entertaining *essentially* the views of *Pre*-millennialists, should *thus mar* that era   he is, we believe, sound and scriptural respecting the Second Advent, but narrows that happy period to a 'shadow or a spectre,' by making it occur *prior* to Christ's Advent!) *That day* which, whenever it arrives, shall come 'as a thief in the night,' may be *close at hand*!!   Could such expressions be used, regarding the consummation, 1,800 years ago; because the final dispensation had set in, and it was "*not given*" *to men to know its duration;* with what *superadded force does the prospect now arise!*" page 39. Again he continues—"We most firmly hold, that man's little ingenuity *may* be altogether at fault in interpreting 'unfulfilled prophecy'!   And that day may overtake us *in a moment*! Watch *therefore*.   Oh Watch! for ye know not *what hour your Lord doth come*. he will at his Second Advent *surprise some*,

even those who are alive and remain   Why should he not surprise *you and me*?
It is the duty of every Christian—the interest—the *only security* of every living
man—to hold himself *each day, each hour* ready for judgment! Death, it is true,
may intervene, but if we are ready for judgment we are ready for death   and if
we are not ready for judgment, O! if he should come and '*not find*' us *watching*''!
(page 40).   With the exception of making the Millennium a mere shadow only
of what we deem that 'good time coming' to be, we would earnestly say—we
would to God that every writer on the *Post*millennial side were as truthful, and
as scriptural as this good man in his views of the Second Advent, and the *importance* of '*watching*' for it!   He does away we see altogether with any creed
which says we have yet *at least a thousand years* to expect.   He will not have his
watching frame of mind thus beguiled.   He does not take up any dream about
Paul knowing the times and the seasons, to shield himself, in being placed
by his views in such a position that obedience to his Lord's command, is
to him a thing impossible'!   He breaks through all Theoretical hindrances—and
stands out boldly with his lamp trimmed—as a man waiting for his Lord's appearing *at any hour*!   We would that the rest of his brethren would cast into the
dust as comparatively worthless, their theories—and their systems—and take up
the Word of God as independent of school notions, and cease to haggle it about, to
make it teach what it was never intended.   If all would put themselves in a
'*waiting*' posture for his Advent at *any hour*—and exhort *the people to do the same*,
instead of drawing off their minds from matter so important, we would cease to
write about the Millennium being *before* or *after* it!   But as long as ever a voice
is heard to tell the people *not* to expect such event, at least before the year 2,856!
we hope at least there will be another, to *drown the echo*! to arrest the cry of
'peace and safety'—by crying aloud and sparing not,—but reiterating again and
again, the Divine counsel—'*watch therefore*, for ye know neither *the day*,
nor *the hour*, wherein the Son of Man Cometh.'   Our brethren indeed may
dilute the binding of Satan, and make it merely nominal, symbolical—but we will
have no such dilution.   They cannot allow it to have its legitimate meaning,
because such would be destructive to their views in other respects   they are so
crippled that they cannot allow Satan's binding to be anything, but a 'figure of
speech,' but we will consent to no such restriction.   He is said to be '*laid hold
of*,'—'*cast into the abyss*,'—'*shut up*'   and then again at the end of the Millennium, '*loosed*' again '*out of his prison*.'   Can such expressions as these be understood as meaning—'that Satan will be under some kind of restraint, so that he

H

will cease to deceive the nations, and yet have his *emissaries* abroad tempting the people " ? To allow anything short of a *personal* restraint, seems to do away with the fact that Satan's binding is a *personal* punishment upon himself! Beside this is treating him just as do Socinians—as a mere influence, we regard such interpretations as destructive to his *personality*! If he be not cast into the abyss in a *personal* sense at the *opening* of the Millennium how can we believe that he will be cast into the lake of fire, in a *personal* sense, when the little season shall have expired—at its *close* ? Mr Lyon too would seem here to put himself in opposition to both Messrs Barnes and Brown; the former says—'his power will be put an end to'; and the latter—'his trade will be put an end to, but Mr. Lyon says—'he will *cease* to deceive the nations, and yet have his *emissaries* abroad *tempting the people*! Now surely if his trade be stopped and if his power be put an end to, his *emissaries* will also be stopped from *tempting the people* ! How the Devil can be said to *cease* to deceive the nations—and yet have his *emissaries* abroad *tempting the people*, we cannot conceive, neither should we think can any other man except Mr. Lyon. But if we take Scripture as our guide, we think surely such an idea seems as false as it appears revolting Look at the 8th chap. of Luke for an all sufficient refutation of such a view " And when he went forth to land, there met him out of the city a certain man which had *devils* long time, &c And Jesus asked him—what is thy name? And he said *legion*, because *many* devils were entered into him, and *they* besought him that he would not command *them* to go *into the abyss*, (εις την αβυσσον) Now be it remembered, this is the same phrase used with regard to Satan, when he is said to be cast into the *bottomless pit* (εις την αβυσσον) at the *opening* of the Millennium; and not the *lake of fire*, into which he is said to be cast at its *close* ! These *emissaries* in number as a legion, were afraid the time had come for being cast with their leader —the Devil, into the (αβυσσον)—abyss; not the *final* place of torment, which is (γεεννα)—the lake of fire. To dispute the *personality* of Satan's binding, and hold such a view as this, would leave the Devil, we should be led to think, in *full power* ! But we hold Scripture teaches the very reverse of this—we have the Devil 'laid hold of,'—'shut up,'—imprisoned; and then afterwards, what might be expected *universal* blessedness resulting from the 'Son of Righteousness' having now arisen in full splendour, and the Devil *ceasing* to go about as a roaring lion seeking whom he may devour ! We however do not so much marvel at our brethren entertaining such antagonistic ideas as the Devil 'ceasing to *decieve the nations*' : and still having his ' *emissaries* abroad *tempting the people*' ! they are, we believe so crippled, that they are straightened to put on even the semblance of consistency.

We come now to the Apocalypse, Rev. 20, a chapter which is said *alone* to favor the idea of two resurrections ; one separate and distinct for the righteous ; but which we totally deny, and maintain this to be the uniform testimony of both Old and New Testament writers ! However if this passage seemed to stand *alone* in our favor here, we would not hesitate in accepting of it then, as long as its plain teaching did not run counter to other parts of inspired Writ. But the doctrine which we here advocate, seems to be so plainly *taught* throughout the entire Bible, that we wonder at the determined opposition to reject it. We have never yet seen an exposition of Rev. 20, apart from the common sense one, which allows common sense phrases—not figurative, to have their obvious literal meaning, that would bear a moment's reflection. Indeed Mr. Lyon would seem to have been highly sensible of this, when he penned these words " *It is not our object so much to interpret Rev. 20, as to show that it does not teach Millenarianism* " ! (page 171). He felt sensible, no doubt, of the difficulty he laboured under here, and beside the danger he would expose himself to, by giving upon his view a *full* exposition of the passage. We think there is much that is prudent here displayed on the part of Mr. Lyon ! He seems fully to have felt the force of our remarks upon phrases having their obvious *natural* meaning.

The substance of his first objection to this chapter teaching a *Pre*millennial resurrection for the righteous, seems to lay in the fact, that *figures* are used in the chapter, and in the book generally. The common place reader however will here observe that such objection vanishes into thin air, when it is marked, that it *equally* applies to Mr. Lyon's own views ! If we are to have the *first* resurrection explained away on this account, we *will* have also the *general* one, so called, explained away ! If the Book being symbolical prevents us from accepting *literally* the *first*, it will *equally* tell against the *general* one ! No objection because of symbols being to be found in the Book, can have any force with us in accepting, or not accepting, of a *first* resurrection *literally ;* unless the same rule be allowed to apply to the *second*, or the *general* resurrection too ! But really Mr. Lyon's arguments upon this chapter are exceedingly futile, they are so opposed to consistency and reason, that one would gladly pass them over. John's description of the *first* resurrection, which he explains in his usual explicative style, " this is the first resurrection," it is said ought not to be *literally* understood, *because* no judicious expounder of God's Word would interpret the following phrases *literally.*   "A white horse"!   "The bottomless pit"!   "The key"!   "The great chain," &c., with the exception, of course, of "*the dead, small and great*"! Now what reasonable man, who wished to get at the truth of Sacred Writ, would really offer such objections?   Indeed, we ought not so much to marvel because if such be not offered, *none can.*   If the *figurative* view of the *first* resurrection be not maintained upon these grounds, it cannot be held at all! We are assured no impartial man, seeking for truth, will accept of such reasoning, as having any force in it. if we contend for what the inspired language seems plainly to teach, we are asked to maintain our position, by *literalizing* all other passages or phrases *unmistakably* figurative: discrimination, the exercise of the judgment of the expositor, in discerning between what is literal and what is figurative, with a fair and honest regard to the context, must be *set aside!*   It is, in fact, the same old foe—on Daniel vii.—we were required to make out 'a figure of representation' to be the 'fact' intended, thereby, to be set forth; or the personality of the Son *visible*, if we could show the *invisible* Father to be *visible!*   On Zec. xiv, too, the same line of argument is used, with respect to the Millenarian interpretation of that passage!   On 2 Thess. ii., 1—8, the same kind of argument also is used; a phrase allowed to mean what the language conveys the idea of, if we could show another phrase capable of bearing a meaning no man ever dared to put upon it.   And now, in this Book of Revelation, we have still to do battle with the same irrational means of warfare, *unmistakably* figurative phrases brought forward to set aside others as *unmistakably* literal if we literalize *anything* opposed to our brethren's school notions, we must literalize *everything!*   We might, indeed, retort, by requesting them to spiritualize or allegorize *everything*, but we only profess to contend for and seek after truth; and we think such retorts would not at all aid us in finding it. Mr. Lyon may ask us to accept in its literal import 'the bottomless pit' and the necessary qualification thereto, *he has specified,*—'a bottomless earth': but we reply, our object *is truth,* and if he requires an *impossibility* shown to be *possible* to convince him, we must leave him where we believe he is,—on the subject of the Second Advent and the two Resurrections,—*in fearful error!*

"I saw the souls of them that were beheaded for the witness of Jesus,—and they lived and reigned with Christ a thousand years.—This is the first resurrection."   'This first resurrection' requires that it should be understood *literally*, not only because of harmony and truths contained in this chapter, but also because a '*first P*remillennial resurrection' is, we think, the uniform testimony of Scripture, " I saw the souls of them that were beheaded, &c." The death here, then, is *no figure*, at least, if so, it is a very stern one ; it rather looks like what we would call a stern reality, if our ideas are at all correct of what we may understand by the phrase 'beheaded.' This, then, being the case, it requires that the resurrection be so too ; this is clear to a *demonstration* ! If the death be *real*, so must the resurrection be *real* ! To maintain the reverse is not only acting contrary to Scripture *precedent*, for in no passage is such a contradiction of ideas to be gathered,—everywhere throughout, Scripture uniformly makes the death either declared or implied to *correspond* with the resurrection : but it also destroyes the meaning of words . The death, here, we say, being *literal*, requires, to a demonstration, that the resurrection be so too, for to suppose otherwise cannot be understood as a resurrection at all !

But again, a resurrection, we think, implies a death previously experienced. In what sense then are we to understand the death of the souls of these Martyrs ? The death of the soul may be said to consist *in the absence of God*. Did God then never quicken the souls of these Martyrs who were beheaded for the witness of Jesus ? This cannot, we are sure, be maintained. Did he then leave them at the stake, or in the flames, or where ? In what sense are their *souls* to be understood as *dead*, and hence need a resurrection ? In what part of their history can we suppose God to have left them and suffered their souls to expire ? Can the soul be said to die in any other sense than in the withdrawal of God's presence ? We ask here to have demonstrated the death of the *soul*, previously implied, which requires, as a consequence, the resurrection of the *spirit*, for which our brethren contend !

If we try to understand this resurrection by *appropriation* or *substitution*, how antagonistic to reason ? How opposed to the rest of the teaching of the Bible ? Let it be granted that John meant a race of men should spring up *like* the Martyrs, after he wrote, what a curious prophecy does it seem ? John says the Martyrs rise from the dead, and he calls this ' *the first* resurrection.' If he meant here a race of men *like* the Martyrs in his time; why then, in the days of Constantine, this *first* resurrection must surely have taken place. Eusebius tells us such was the *revival* of Martyr principles then, that the Christians went home, chanting songs of praise to God; and, indeed, so much like a *revival* of Martyr principles was this, that many looked upon it as the *beginning of the Millennium* ! The Millennium then, as Mr. Waldegrave holds, and whose work Mr. Lyon recommends as containing the *same views as he himself entertains*, may be said to have *terminated with the Reformation!* Martin Luther, Melancthon, &c., then, in such a case, may be said to stand as the representatives of Mr. Lyon's ' *Second* figurative resurrection,' who spring up at the end of the Millennium, and almost *extinguish real Christianity* ' ! How true the sentiment of Hooker here—" There is nothing more *dangerous* than this *licentious art,* which changeth the meaning of words, maketh of anything what it listeth, and, in the end bringeth *all truth to nothing* " ! Depend upon it, when we wander away from God's plain revelation and take up with our own fanciful notions instead, we shall at last find that his word, instead of being a light unto our feet and a lamp unto our path, will become, in the place thereof, *a dark lantern!* If, again, we take this resurrection in the sense of *substitution* and pass over the days of Constantine, why then, surely, it took place *in the days of Martin Luther* ! The Millennium began at the Reformation, and we may *dispense* with all the injunctions ' *to watch,*' for the Second Coming of Christ, enjoined upon us, for, at least, *six or seven hundred years to come!* and we may look out, according to *Anti*-Millenarians, for a period of *unparalleled* wickedness, in the shape of Apostasy, which will almost *extinguish* the blessed Millennial happiness the world *now* enjoys— i e ' *Nations not lifting up sword against nations, &c.*' ' *All knowing the Lord, from the least to the greatest*' ! If, again, we take this resurrection in the sense of *substitution,* and look forward for this race of men, *like* the Martyrs, to spring up ; why then it will be the *third* instead of the *first* resurrection ! Beside, how opposed to reason, ' *Martyrs*' mean ' *men in the flesh,*' who never could have suffered ' *Martyrdom,*' ! ' *Martyr spirits*' mean ' *men in bodily form*' and yet be called a *spiritual* resurrection ! Who can understand these things ? If, as Mr. Lyon says, ' ignorance at Rome is the mother of devotion' surely *ignorance* here will be essential to *compliance* ! Moreover, as a very large number of *Anti*-Millenarians are now compelled to admit ' if we apply this process of *substitution* to the *first* resurrection, and to the *second* resurrection, we must also apply it to the *general judgment!* What *other* race of men then did John mean by ' *the dead small and great*' ? What *other* sea—by *the* sea ? What *other* death—by *death?* What *other* hades—by *Hades?* What *other* lake of fire— by *the* lake of fire ' What *other* second death—by *the* second death ? Can *such* idea or principle of interpretation be at all tolerated ?

Mr. Lyon's argument about ' souls' being the symbol only of the resurrection of the Martyrs, because the ' seven candlesticks' were the symbol of the ' seven churches' is very futile. As in all his other arguments about ' figures' requiring to be made 'facts,' the same fallacy is apparent here on the very surface. The 'seven candlesticks' could *not*, in any sense, be understood as the *fact* itself.—i e, 'seven churches,'—while they can be understood as very apt emblems, and as they are explained to be the '*figures*' of them. With respect to the expression 'souls,' we say it *can* be understood as the *fact* itself,—i.e, the resurrection of the body, while it *canno* be understood as the '*figure*' only, because it is explained as the '*fact*' itself. The use of a *figure* to shadow forth a thing signified, which signification is, after all, to be only a *figure*, is an anomaly, the like of which no man ever heard. Mr. Lyon's *figurative* resurrection is, after all, only a *figure;* hence his 'seven candlesticks' symbolizing 'seven churches,' ought not to stop here, but the 'seven churches' ought to symbolize something else! We may here retort upon him then, in his own words used upon this very point, respecting Messrs Birks and Bonar. 'We marvel at his blindness in using such argument!'

The expression 'Souls' everybody knows is a phrase as common to Jewish writers as any provincialism now going, and signifies generally both soul and body —the entire man. We read of eight *souls* saved in the Ark, will Mr. Lyon here tell us eight *souls* were not eight *bodies*, but only the *symbol* of them ? Will he here tell us the *soul* merely was *saved from drowning* ? We read of *souls* in Nineveh, and *souls* in Paul's ship; if this Hebraistic phrase, it be contended, applies *only* to the soul in Rev. xx. 4, we ask how, as in these phrases and many more we could add, can it be said to be capable of death ? If in Revelations it can be said to rise from the dead, surely in the above cases it may equally be restricted to the spirit of man, and we may suppose that the *soul* in an absolute sense was saved from *drowning* in the above case! Indeed we wonder at Mr. Lyon at all contending for a *figurative* resurrection of the Martyrs—when there are so many of his brethren *Post*millenarians, who fully admit such a position to be quite *untenable*. Mr. Cobbin, to whom we have already referred, may be said to stand as the representative of a very large class, who although not Millenarians, fully allow of a *literal* resurrection of the Martyrs, a thousand years before the wicked. He remarks upon Rev. xx 4.—"I saw the souls" *the persons*, (not their spirits, as Mr Lyon contends for merely) And they lived and reigned, &c It is not said they reigned on the earth, and as the bodies of saints arose at the resurrection of Jesus, (Matthew xxvii, 52, 53.) So may these be with Christ.... Others say a generation of men *like the Martyrs* will spring up, as John the Baptist came in the spirit and power of Elijah... the question is, are we to understand the description *literally* or *figuratively?* If figuratively—*then the General Resurrection can* only *be understood figuratively, as a Spiritual Resurrection*!! If the '*Martyrs*' rise only in a *spiritual* sense, then '*the rest of the dead*' rise only in a *spiritual sense,* but if the '*rest of the dead*' rise *really*—the '*Martyrs*' rise *in the same manner*! The symbolic language used in connection with this prediction, would induce us not to take them *literally; but then the same argument would apply to the General Judgment and Resurrection*!! 'The rest of the dead lived not again,' until, &c..this seems to justify the opinion, the first resurrection of the *bodies* of the *Martyred* Saints!" We marvel that Mr. Lyon should contend for what even *Anti* Millenarians say is *untenable,* for his making out '*the rest of the dead*' figurative; and the *general judgment* literal, as Mr Cobbin observes very justly, is a thing that cannot be done! The very same argument is most powerfully maintained by that accomplished writer, Professor Stuart, see his Comment upon this passage; and also Excursus vi. (v. ii. p. 476) We have no doubt but these good men will eventually give up the *Post*millennial Advent; *four* Resurrections are unwarrantable,—the '*Martyrs*' must be associated with *Christ's* at his coming!!

The objection that '*Martyred*' saints are only to rise, supposing now 'this first resurrection' to be proved literal, has no force in it John depicts the group of the redeemed by selecting out the most distinguished from among them—like a general at the head of an army, he places first and foremost 'the noble army of martyrs'! It is said 'they lived and reigned with Christ a thousand years'—then Christ was among the risen although *not* mentioned! But I see no reason why this phrase '*beheaded*' should be so rigidly restricted to Martyrdom, as πελεκιζω from πελεκυς an axe,) if strictly held, must signify that kind of beheading with *an axe,* common to the Romans. Certainly *some* of the early *Martyrs* may have suffered thus; but it cannot be maintained that *all* did. If then this phrase can be extended to *every* kind of Martyrdom; why may it not embrace the *whole* body of Christ? Like Paul, each disciple is called upon 'to suffer the loss of *all* things,'—and it has always been true,—"They that will live godly in Christ Jesus shall suffer persecution." The latter part of this 4th verse referring more particularly to Papal and not Pagan Rome, would seem to justify the idea—that John here meant *every* individual who had continued 'faithful unto death.' 'Who had not worshiped the Beast,' &c. See Rev xiii. 8. *All* are meant, 'whose names *are* written in the Lamb's Book of Life.' If, however it be still maintained that '*Martyrs*' *only* are meant, we reply then, that such scrupulous persons will put themselves in scrupulous circumstances, where perhaps they would rather be less scrupulous. For example, in another part of this Book, the number sealed, is said to be 144,000. Those who say we shall not *exceed* the number specified in our *first* resurrection; must also be prepared to put their *seal* upon the 144,000, and not allow of *any addition !* But the only fair way is to interpret Scripture by Scripture, and we have only to turn to Paul to help out the meaning of John, and we have our point clearly proved. See 1 Thes. iv. 16. " *The* dead in Christ, shall rise *first* " Here we gather the idea that *the* dead— the *whole* family of God—not *a part* merely; rise in the '*first* resurrection' ! And has this resurrection of Paul's in this passage nothing to do with John's? To what resurrection then does it belong?—Mr Lyon's *general* one? What then can Paul mean by *the* dead *in Christ* (only), rising *first* ?' Let Mr Lyon reconcile this statement with his idea, of the dead *in Christ*, and the dead *out of Christ* rising *at the same time* !!

But, again, John says the righteous shall rise at the *opening* of the Millennium, that is at the Coming of Christ to *introduce* it! Then we have the same testimony given us by Paul, in 1 Cor xv, 23 —" But every man in his own order, Christ the first-fruits, afterward they that *are Christ's* at his *Coming.*" Does not this passage also teach the same truth, that of two *separate* and distinct resurrections? A resurrection for the 'righteous' *only* at Christ's *coming* ? Will Mr Lyon here contend in *this order* that Christ is not *now* risen? Upon what grounds then can he contend for they who '*are Christ's*,' and they who are ' *not Christ's* to rise at the *same time ?* Who authorized Mr. Lyon to break ' *this order* ' of the inspired Apostle ? 'Christ the firstfruits'—then they who ' *are* Christ's *only* ' at his coming ' Can no sober mind here gather the idea, that the saints will rise a thousand years *before* the wicked? How will Mr. Lyon in his sober moments reconcile the Apostle's *order*,—they 'who are Christ's' *only* when he *comes ;* with his idea of they 'who *are* Christ's' and they who are *not*, at the *same time ?*

Again in the 49th Psalm, I think we have a clear and decided reference to the doctrine of a *separate* resurrection for the righteous—it is said, the wicked are laid in the grave like sheep, and 'death shall feed on them,'—i e. continue to rot, but "the *upright* shall have dominion over them *in the morning*"! 'The upright,' the *righteous* shall in the day of the Son of Man, have dominion 'over the *wicked*' in the morning—the Millennial morning! 'The *upright*' shall be redeemed from the power of the grave; in this *order* i.e. in the *first* resurrection ; while the

J

grave shall still *continue* to be a *habitation for the wicked*' In the 149 Psalm we have Paul's account of the first resurrection for the righteous in this passage of Corinthians also confirmed, "let the saints be joyful in glory....to execute vengeance upon the heathen, and punishment upon the people.. to execute upon them the *judgments written*, this honor have *all his saints*" If *all* his saints have ' *this honour*,' why then they must *all* be raised *prior* to the *wicked* at the last judgment that awaits the world! Couple with this idea Paul's declarations already adverted to—especially the former one in Thessalonians, there we have an account of his Second Advent, the '*risen saints*' joining him, and then those found living 'caught up also to meet the Lord in the air.' Couple again this chapter and the 149th Psalm as alluded to, with our remarks upon Zech 14, and Daniel 7. 'And the Lord my God shall come, and *all his saints with him*,' &c. See how this idea -*uniformly* taught in Scripture dovetails with the accounts of the two resurrections given by the respective writers ' '*All* shall be made alive,' says Paul, but 'every man in his *own order*,'—'Christ the firstfruits,'—'*Now* is Christ risen from the dead and become the firstfruits of them that slept,'—his resurrection then *is passed* —next comes in *this order*, ' they who *are Christ's* at his coming, and at that period *only* they —and finally will the wicked have their turn—in the *evening ;* the righteous have dominion in the *morning*—i.e. the *opening* of the Millennium—the wicked shall rise in the *evening*—after its *close*,—' for *all* shall be made alive. In the 25th chap. of Isaiah the same idea is conveyed—"He will *swallow up death in victory*, and the Lord God will wipe away tears from off all faces ; *and the rebuke of his people shall he take away* from off all the earth ; for the Lord hath spoken it." This seems to refer to the conversion of the Jews, when the ' *veil shall be taken away*' of which Paul speaks in 2 Cor. iii. 12—16. And the Resurrection of the just, as alluded to in 1 Cor. xv. 51—57. "We shall not all sleep, but we shall *all* be changed, &c ... for this *corruptible* shall put on *incorruption*, &c.... then shall be brought to pass the saying that is written (in Isaiah xxv. 8.)—*Death is swallowed up in victory*" " The Prophet here confirms this *Pre*millennial Resurrection; and also by *associating with it* the conversion of the Jews—confirms the *Pre*millennial Advent—for he adds " And it shall be said *in that day*,' (the day of his Coming'—of the resurrection of the righteous,—of the changing of living,—and of the conversion of the Jews,) ' Lo this is our God, we have *waited for him*," (just what Paul commanded the Thessalonians to do—' *wait for Christ*') and he will save us ; this is the Lord, we have *waited for him*, we will be glad and rejoice in his salvation." Also in the 26th chap. of Isaiah, the Prophet speaking of the *wicked* says—" they *are dead*, they shall *not live* they *are deceased*, they shall *not rise*," the Prophet here could not refer to the *General* Resurrection, when *all* shall awake ' but evidently to *that first* and better one, in which they who *are Christ's only*, shall partake ! Again in the 19th verse, he speaks of his body the church '—rising. " Thy dead men shall live, together with my dead body shall they arise, awake and sing ye that dwell in dust, for thy dew is as the dew of herbs, and the earth shall cast out the dead." If the Prophet be understood as speaking here in his own person, the sense is—" that *thy* dead shall rise ' together with ' me ", but if this declaration be understood as the Lord speaking of his church, then the words ' together with,' which are not in the original, should be omitted, and the sense would be something like this,—' my dead body—' the church ' shall arise.' However, in any case, there would seem here reference to be made to the ' resurrection of the *righteous*,' which is distinct from that of the wicked ! In Dan. xii. 2 also, the same great truth is intimated. "And *many of them* (evidently not all at the same time) that sleep in the dust of the earth shall awake, some (literally *these*) to everlasting life, and some (literally *those*) to everlasting shame and contempt." Here again there seems to be reference made to the ' deliverance of Israel' and the '*first* resurrection'—as events *contemporaneous* ' Mr Lyon mentions this passage to show that two resurrections separated by a thousand years, is inconsistent with Daniel's teaching. He has not however said in what sense it is inconsistent with a *Pre*millennial resurrection, nor yet in what sense it can be made to teach his own idea of one *general* resurrection for both righteous and wicked at the *end of the Millennium !* There is a cautiousness about Mr. Lyon upon this point of the controversy that would seem to say—he felt he was upon *uncertain* and *slippery* ground ! Some writers before him have objected to our acceptation of Daniel's referring to a Premillennial resurrection, because he uses the prefatory sentence —' at that time,'—Now if it be objected—" the many *from among* or *of them* that sleep "—refers to such resurrection because of—' at that time '—it would seem to us entirely destructive to the opposite view. "At that time,' shall Michael stand up, the great Prince, which standeth for the children of thy people · and there shall be a time of trouble, such as never was since there was a nation, even to that same time, and ' at that time ' *thy people shall be delivered*, every one that shall be found written in the Book, and *many of them* that sleep shall awake, &c." Here we think reference is made to the great and unprecedented calamity that awaits the world *prior* to, and accompanying the Second Advent, which will usher in the *National* conversion of the Jew, 'that time when thy people shall be delivered'—and 'a nation be born in a day.' See also by way of confirmation of this, Jer. xxx 7. Isa xxv 6—8. compared with 1 Cor xv. 51—57 2 Cor. iii. 12—16. Rom. xi 25-27. Rev xxi 4. So that if we are denied a *Premillennial* resurrection here, I think we must also be *denied* a *Premillennial deliverance of Israel !* Will our brethren have then their Millennium to themselves? Will they *exclude* the poor Jew from participating in its blessings, few indeed as they would make them out to be? Will they have 'Israel's' deliverance only *at the time* of the *general* resurrection? We think the poor Jew has already suffered sufficiently at the merciless hands of many of the followers of Origen, allegorising, and appropriating to themselves Jewish promises, never intended for the Gentile church, until both Jew and Gentile shall become one fold under one shepherd ! We deny not the spiritual blessing for the Gentile, which must of necessity flow from the *natural* and *physical* blessings intended *primarily* for the Jew; but we do protest against that selfish, and ungenerous mediœval fallacy,—Gentiles appropriating to themselves *all* the poor Jew's blessings, and leaving him to the bitter relishing of the curses only ! In John v 28, 29 the same truth is taught, that of two *separate* and *distinct* resurrections "The hour is coming, in which all that are in their graves shall hear his voice, and shall come forth, they that have done good unto the resurrection of life, and they that have done evil unto the resurrection of damnation" Mr Lyon has not said here again in what sense this passage cannot refer to two separate and distinct resurrections with a thousand years between. We may however remark, that if this and the passage in Daniel, we have just noticed, be the strongholds of our brethren, they must, we think, to every unprejudiced mind appear very *weak* ! If they are necessitated to take up a mere general statement in the abstract, to argue against the most clear, definite, and unmistakable teaching of other portions of Divine Writ,—we would not give much for their *ground to stand upon*! Here our Lord merely asserts a fact, that *all* will rise, and that some will come forth to the 'resurrection of life"—and that some will come forth to the 'resurrection of damnation' He does not state that *all* will awake at the *same* moment ! on the contrary, no intelligent reader acquainted with the signification generally of the term, 'hour,' 'day,' 'season,' &c. in Scripture, would for a moment suppose such a thing. The specification of some to 'the resurrection of life'; and some to 'the resurrection of damnation'—would lead the majority of readers to believe John here meant *two* separate and distinct resurrections. and when they looked at the passage, in the light of his teaching more *minutely* in Rev. 20, and in the light of Paul's general teaching, we think the conclusion with ninety-nine out of every hundred would be *inevitable*! The exploded argument about the term—'hour,' ($\omega\rho\alpha$) will not support Mr. Lyon's assertion, that this passage cannot teach two resurrections with a thousand years between. It can embrace two with a thousand years between, just as easily as '*the day* of Salvation' can be understood to have *now* lasted some *Millenaries!* But there is a passage in John's First Epistle (ii. 18) that entirely dissipates every shade of argument here, that can be brought forward against two separated by a thousand years. "Little children it is the *last time* ($\omega\rho\alpha$) and as ye have heard that Antichrist shall come, even now are there many Antichrist's, whereby we know that it is the *last time*" ($\omega\rho\alpha$)! Now this selfsame disputed word is here used by John twice repeated, and it *has had reference already to* 1,800 *years!* The argument about *a thousand years* then is dissipated. But then many imagine, I think, very foolishly and unwarrantably, that '*the day* of judgment'—will be a day of twenty-four hours. "But of that *day* and *hour* knoweth no man,"—i e. when Christ shall come to judgment. We are not here to understand *literally* this *day* and *hour!* Take another passage, "Behold now is the accepted *time*, now is the *day* of Salvation."—"In the *day* that God made the earth and the heaven." '*Time*,' '*hour*,' '*day*,' then most generally mean— 'a season,'—so will the 'day of judgment' be a season, and so will the resurrection of both righteous and wicked, be *a season*, bounded alike by the Advent of Christ at the *opening* of the Millennium, and the final act of judgment upon the guilty—who shall be raised from their graves after its *close*, thus the time or '*the hour*' of the resurrection and of judgment, will be at least a thousand years. But again, the fact of John's employing here for his 'resurrection of *damnation*' the same kind of phraseology he employs with regard to *all in* the so called *general* resurrection, looks very *suspicious!* He says here 'some will come forth unto the resurrection of *damnation*,' or condemnation. In Rev. xx. 12 he says—all '*every man* was judged (i.e. we think *condemned*) according to his works"! How then is it, we ask, that *all* in the *general* resurrection are said to be *judged* or *condemned*, in the same kind of phraseology used in the Gospel for those *only* who have '*done evil*'? What is the difference between a resurrection of *condemnation*,' and 'a resurrection in which all are *judged* or *condemned?* Is there any *condemnation* to them who are in Christ Jesus? Paul says *there is not!* John says also again and again *there is not!*

Hear him—" He that heareth my words **and** believeth on him that sent me, hath everlasting life, and shall *not come into condemnation,*" (judgment with the wicked) John v. 24. " He that believeth is *not condemned* " John iii. 18. How could John use the same verb with regard to *all* in one place ; and again say in another place that it should not apply to *any* who were believers in Christ, and yet mean it *indiscriminately* to refer to both ? We hold with ' *no judgment* ' in the sense given of it in Rev. xx. 12. for the righteous hereafter. The judgment of the righteous will consist in giving *reward* ! A very different *assize* from that which will consign men to everlasting destruction for the rejection of Christ ! The believer has no such assize to enter, we think, after death, ' Being *justified* (now) by his grace he has peace with God '—' There is therefore *now* no *condemnation* to them which are in Christ Jesus,'—' who shall lay *anything* to the charge of God's elect '—' It is God that justifieth *(now)* who is he then that shall condemn, or even judge him *hereafter ?* He rests *now* on the Rock of Ages, and his safety is *absolute*—no precariousness about him, he is as unassailable—as unalterable, as the hand that wrote his name in the Book of life of the *Lamb slain from the foundation of the world.* Again, we would ask how is it that *no mention* is made of the *righteous* in the so called *general* resurrection ? How is it that *nothing* is said about reward ? What ! does God take more pleasure in *wrath* than *mercy ; condemnation* than *justification ; punishment* than *reward ?* that he should tell us *all* about ' *every man* ' being judged according to his works ; and say *nothing* about ' *any man* ' being *rewarded* ' ! Oh ! may it be ours to rise and be ' *recompensed* at the resurrection of the *just* ' ! See Luke xiv. 14. How is it, we repeat the question, that no mention is made in the *general* resurrection of this ' *recompense* of the *just* '? If we may be allowed to answer this question—It was as John plainly tells us—because ' the righteous were raised a thousand years *prior* to this,' in the *first* resurrection ! It was because those who ' come *not into condemnation* ' were raised at the *opening* of the Millennium ! It was because they had ' dominion over the wicked in the morning ' of the Millennium ! It was because they were previously raised and made partakers in that ' *first* and better resurrection spoken of in Heb. xi. 35. It was because ' they were thought worthy to obtain *that* world, and *that* resurrection *from among* the dead ' in Luke xx. 35 ! It was because they *attained* unto *that* resurrection which Paul was so anxious to reach !—' If by any means I might attain unto *that* resurrection *from among* the dead,' Phil. iii. 11. Did the Apostle *strive* for that which he could *not* possibly *miss ?* If there were only one *general* resurrection, what could Paul *strive* for? What did he mean by *that* resurrection? Was it not John's *first*, that upon the partakers of which, the second death can have no power? Upon the principle of one *general* resurrection, the Apostle's words are *unintelligble!*

Now we think Mr Lyon has got a good deal of *literalism* to give up in all these passages we have just glanced at—as much to make them fit and square with his system, as will counterbalance by more than a thousand to one his vague objection made to our view—because of Matt. xxvi. 64. "Hereafter ye shall see the Son of Man sitting on the right hand of power, and coming in the clouds of heaven." This passage we are informed has never been reconciled with a *Pre*millenarian creed, and seems to present to Mr Lyon the greatest obstacle to the doctrine of a *Pre*millennial resurrection! We propose therefore to make a few observations upon it, and see whether it teaches our view, or that of Mr. Lyon. It is contended in the first place, that the Jewish High Priest and Council who put the Son of God to death *must* be raised in that *Pre*millenial resurrection, in order to '*see* the Son of Man coming in the clouds of heaven'! Well, and suppose this to be the case, what of that? Will Mr Lyon here step forward and say such upon the *Pre*millenial view *cannot* be the case? Will he dare arbitrarily to say that the Jewish High Priest and Council died at last impenitent? How does he know this? What right has man to *suppose* such a case? Beside is it not only *possible* but even highly *probable*, that these men were among those who Peter *afterwards* 'pricked to the heart'? It is not very probable we say, that they were among those whom Peter accused, when he said—"He being delivered by the determinate council and foreknowledge of God, *ye* have taken and by wicked hands *have crucified and slain*"? But this is speculative, we can, we think, afford to be independent of speculation here, although this conjecture is not without considerable weight, and very allowable; at any rate we have as much right to claim it as Mr Lyon!! But cannot we show this passage to be *consistent* with our views upon another foundation, quite independent of any speculation? The reconciliation we think perfectly easy, in fact there is nothing to reconcile. The passage has only to be understood in the light that similar phrases are, and must be accepted and it is seen fully to corroborate our views, while it cuts up and shivers to pieces those of Mr. Lyon! The fallacy of his reasoning lays in the idea, that Christ referred *alone* or *absolutely* to the Jewish High Priest and Council *then* living; a few observations, will show this to be wrong.—In Mark 13, He told his disciples that he was like a man going into a far country, to seek for himself a kingdom and to return for which period he commanded his servants.

'to watch'—'Watch *ye* for that period, lest coming suddenly I find *you* sleeping' —'What I say unto *you* I say unto *all* watch.' Now Mr. Lyon asks—"Will Millenarians *gravely* affirm that Christ's words (in Matt xxvi 64) should be paraphrased thus—I say unto you, hereafter shall *ye* (that is the Jews who shall be living some 1,800 years hence,) hereafter shall *ye* (that is *they*) see the Son of Man coming in the clouds of heaven"? (page 171) To meet this enquiry, we may ask another question. 'Will Mr. Lyon *gravely* affirm, that the above passage in Mark 13, and many similar ones to be found in Holy Writ, do *not* apply to those who live *some* 1,800 *years after their utterance* ? Will he tell us *ye*, in that case does *not* refer, or apply to *they* ? Will he dare to say that Christ in commanding *ye* to watch for his return, did *not* command *us* – i e *they* ? What then does he mean by bringing forward such a vague objection as this, to the acceptation of the *Premillennial* resurrection ? He overlooks here the great and important fact, that Christ spoke of his Second Advent, as if it would occur, in the time of those *then* living! as if it were *at hand* ! The argument here is founded upon the mistaken notion, that Christ and his disciples spoke to the generation then living, as if they knew, or intended to make them understand, that it would not occur until some period in the *far distant* future ; whereas the reverse is the case, they always crushed such a notion with representing that event as taking place at *any* time, to be looked for at *any* hour, that they should 'watch' for his coming as if it concerned them only ! This passage then instead of being against us, is for us, it corroborates our views while it cuts up and dissipates those of Mr Lyon, which teach that we should look for such event *after* the expiration of a *defined* Millenary ! It teaches our view of looking for Christ at *any* period; while it scatters to to the winds the notion, that he cannot come until the Millennium has expired, and thus make obedience to his commands *a thing impossible* to all preceding generations ! But again had Christ here in view that of teaching anything about the nature of his Second Advent in particular— or of the resurrection of the body ? We must consult the context, and ascertain what was the nature of his argument here, in order to judge correctly of its bearing upon the doctrine of a *Premillennial* resurrection. for if we take up '*observations*' without their connection, or reference to the context—what *contradictions may we not find?* Then the subject matter before the High Priest and Council, was that of his *Sonship*,—whether he was the '*Son of God*'; this was the occasion of his remark—'Hereafter ye shall see the Son of Man sitting on the right hand of power, and coming in the clouds of heaven.' And what, we may ask, has this got to do with the *Premillennial* resurrection? What has it got to do with the fact of those whom he addressed rising or not *in that resurrection*? Nothing whatever. These remarks of Christ were only made to declare his '*Sonship*,'—his '*Majesty*,'—that although he was then about to be crucified as a man,—yet '*hereafter*' he would be seen 'coming in the clouds of heaven' as the *Son of God*—and the *judge of the world*! That he had in view no intention of teaching anything about either the resurrection of the body—or the time specially of his Advent, is seen from the account given of the same by Luke, who *overlooks altogether*, the fact of '*his coming*,' and mentions *only* that which he evidently had in view—that of *asserting* his '*Sonship*,'—" Hereafter shall ye see the Son of Man sitting on the right hand of power." Not a word about his 'coming in the clouds of heaven'!! We have then no right to take this passage, and tare it away from the context, to make it speak, what it was never intended. If we want to get at the truth of the doctrine of the resurrection of the body, we must take those passages which treat of it *specially*, and not carry observations and 'exhortations' *beyond the grave*, that were never intended so to apply; these observations were for the *living*—not the *dead*! Mr. Lyon has no more right to make these words refer to the Jewish High Priest and Council *alone* or *after* death, than he has to maintain that the observations—" Then shall *ye* begin to say "—or " I tell *you* I know *you* not "—apply *alone*, or exclusively, and *after* death, to those *identical* persons who interrogated our Lord on that occasion! Or he has as much right to arbitrate upon the *final* state of those men being *justified* or *condemned* our Lord addressed in (Matt. xxvi. 64.) as he has to affirm that those who questioned him (the *ye*) just now adverted to, were found at last amongst those who '*enter not in*' : and were not partakers consequently in the *Premillennial* resurrection, or *at* his coming!!

After our remarks upon so many passages teaching his personal reign upon the earth, we think it quite unnecessary to take up his observation—that supposing the *Premillennial* resurrection now proved; the *locality* of their reign with Christ, as being *the Earth*, is not specified. We have shown this to be so over and over again; however we will just add one more quotation, which teaches this *literally* and *demonstrably*. In Rev. v. 9, 10, we read of a company redeemed—" Out of every kindred, and tongue, and people, and nation " ; made kings and priests unto God : and they say—" we *shall* reign —where? in heaven. no, " we *shall* reign *on the Earth*!!

K

Mr. Lyon observes—that we must be put to sad shifts to prove a *literal* reign, when we quote this passage in Rev. v. 10.' We think we can understand perfectly the latent meaning of his observation; no doubt it is a hard passage, needing a '*sad shift*,' on his part, to prove that it can teach a *spiritual* reign! We dont wonder at him stumbling here with a *murmur* only—*a mere passing allusion!* Many as are the passages from which a *literal* reign can be proved, no doubt this is one of the worst *spiritualizers* have got to deal with! Daniel's *earthly* kingdom of Messiah, &c., they think they can get over; and they try hard by *appropriation, substitution*, &c. &c. to make the first resurrection and reign of Christ in Rev. 20 *spiritual*. But here the song of the Lamb is taken up by the redeemed *out of every kindred, and tongue, and people, and nation*, made kings and priests unto God, and they say—we shall reign *on the earth!* This is a hard passage for our brethren, the number of the redeemed here would seem to be *too large*, not to mean more than *Martyrs*, as they contend for in Rev. 20. hence '*Martyr principles*' substituted for '*Martyrs indeed*' would seem to be somewhat *inappropriate* here! The 'four and twenty elders' say—'we shall reign *on the earth*, but how can this be understood *spiritually?* What can be the *spiritual* meaning of those redeemed out of *every kindred*, &c. saying—we shall reign *on the earth?* Christ, we are told, will not *literally* reign *on the earth*, during the Millennium—'they lived and reigned with Christ a thousand years,'—means—that Christ will be *in heaven* and the Martyrs *in heaven*: but their *principles* upon *the earth!* But the *whole* redeemed family of God represented here by the 'four and twenty elders'—say 'we shall reign *on the earth!* Does this mean their *principles* will be *on the earth*, and their bodies or their souls *in heaven*, if so, we ask, what *race of beings* on earth, may we suppose to inhabit their *principles?* If it be disputed that they do not typify the *whole* Family of God—we ask how they can be said to reign *on the earth*, and *in heaven* at the same time? Christ we are told will be *in heaven*, the 'four and twenty elders' then must be *separated* from him, unless they can be shown to be *ubiquitous!* Would the *spiritual* view be—'absent from the body and *present* with the Lord'—in such a case? Mr. Lyon affects to treat this passage as nothing in the way of his theory, and yet he can find only *one* objection to our view of it, without at the same time showing *how he can interpret it himself*—he asks—'will (Millenarians maintain that the four-beasts (*living creatures* properly) are *literally* to reign *on the earth*'? We might here reply *yes*, if he can show they are *literally* 'four beasts'! He appears to have overlooked the fact, that these 'four living creatures' are not generally understood to say, with the elders—'we shall reign *on the earth.*' This song of the *redeemed* according to Dr. Woodhouse, and we might say the majority of critics is *confined* to the elders; and only joined by the 'four living creatures' in the chorus, as seen in the concluding verse of the chapter. "And the four living creatures said—Amen'! In none of the preceding or following chapters do they seem to claim the character of the *redeemed*, as expressed in the song of the 'four and twenty elders' consequently they are not to be understood as saying with the elders—'we shall reign *on the earth*,'—but only to add their *Amen* to it! Mr. Lyon should have shown us how these 'four living creatures,' understood generally to typify some order of angelic intelligences, could say—'thou hast *redeemed* us to God *by thy blood*,'—he would then have seemed to have some better ground for asking—' are they *literally* to reign *on the* earth! If he cannot show them to be of the *redeemed*, he cannot show that they take part in the song of those who say 'we shall reign *on the earth!* If he can show they are of the *redeemed*, then we say—'*they will reign on the earth*! We think Mr Lyon committed a slight mistake, when he said—" These words are *part* of the song of the '*four living creatures!!*

With respect to Millenarianism in its practical tendency Mr. Lyon says—'No error can be harm*less*,' hence we think the foregoing pages show *his* views to be harm*ful*. Indeed it would seem that he himself felt compelled to admit this in some sense when he penned these words—" Millenarians *have rendered an important service to the church*,' by directing attention to the *prominence* which the inspired writings give to the Second Advent"! 'As no error can be harm*less*, we say it follows from the vast '*practical good*' resulting from Millenarianism, which Mr. Lyon allows, that it must be *beneficial—truthful*! And the opposite which has *suffered loss* by not seeing this *prominence* given by Scripture to the Second Advent, must be *detrimental—harmful*. But in addition to this vast advantage in a practical point of view, Millenarianism is already seen to have conceded in its favor. Which is preeminently the advocate of the Bible? A few considerations based upon the great and important fact—that '*All* Scripture is given by inspiration of God, and is *profitable*,' will show, we think, a further advantage on the side of Millenarianism.

FIRST. '*Anti*-millenarians often tell us that this '*prominent*' doctrine of the Second Advent, although in the Bible, is '*not essential to Salvation;* and therefore not deemed a *practical* subject' Mr. Lyon holding professedly the *prominence* of such doctrine of Holy Writ, and many things we are really pleased to find, of course may be said to be somewhat exceptional, although really and truly placed in such circumstances with his views of it, that this prominence must be next akin to the views contained in the proposition we have laid down. But the objection to the doctrine of the Second Advent, as being ' *not essential* to salvation,' is very common among *Anti*-millenarians, and hence it is put aside as *not practical*! Now can it be that God should falsify himself, by giving to man a revelation of himself--his works—and his ways, professedly for his *better* guidance, and yet mean that much of it is to be deemed—*not practical*—of no *utility*? How contrary to this, the many plain express declarations of his word—'*all* Scripture is *profitable*'! '*Whatsoever* things were written aforetime, were written for our *learning*,' that we through patience and comfort of the Scriptures might have *hope*'! '*All*,' '*whatsoever*,' these terms seem to have too wide a grasp, not to take in the doctrine of the Second Advent. Ah but, say some, you include much therein yet—'*unfulfilled*.' We must let that alone *until* it is *fulfilled*. And what, we might ask, will be the *practical* use of Prophecy relating to the Second Advent when *fulfilled*? What use the dim *star*-light of Prophecy when the *Sun* himself shall have arisen in full noon-day splendour? But Peter says—'We have a more sure word of Prophecy, whereunto we do well to take heed *until* the day dawn'! Not useful *after* the day has dawned! But *now* useful, *until* the day dawn! It is to be of *practical utility*, while the night is spending: not when the day not far distant, shall have come to hand. But how such idea is crushed in the exordium to the *most difficult* book in the Bible,—'*Blessed* is he that *readeth*, and they that *hear* the words of this Prophecy, and *keep* those things which are written therein." But it may still be added, salvation does not depend upon these after all. Salvation is of grace no doubt—not of works, nor of any amount of information the head may contain—but is the Bible written *only* for the *bare* salvation of men? Hear the Apostle Paul rebuke most fearfully this notion—" For when for the time ye ought to be teachers, ye have need that one teach you, which be the first principles of the oracles of God and are become such as have need of milk and not of strong meat, for everyone that useth milk, is *unskilful* in the word of righteousness—*for he is a babe* "! therefore he continues ' *leaving* the first principles (things only necessary to salvation) of the doctrine of Christ let us go on into *perfection*'! see Heb. v., 12—14, &c. It is needless to follow out this unfounded notion, which has taken possession of so many minds, but we would here ask,—is it the offshoot of Millenarianism, or *Anti*-Millenarianism? It is not of the former but of the latter, for such sentiments as these Millenarians have now to do battle with, in meeting those of the opposite side!

SECOND   *Anti*-Millenarians often tell us—'unfulfilled prophecy' is not for man to understand *until* its *accomplishment*, when it will then minister to our faith,—show us how faithful God is in *performing* his *promises.*' This is founded very much upon the same ideas as the foregoing proposition, and we need only revert to our remarks thereupon, to see how utterly unfounded and *anti*-scriptural such sentiments are   How do they comport with John's preface to the Book of Revelations *unfulfilled*? We might ask how can they be harmonized with many similar portions of Holy Writ, but this is quite unnecessary. Peter says—Prophecy is of *use* not *after* its fulfilment· but *until* it is accomplished! 'Minister to our faith, by showing us how faithful God has been in performing his promises' What is faith? Paul says, 'the substance of things *hoped for*— the evidence of things *not seen*'! Hope that *is seen*, is *not* hope—what a man *seeth* why doth he yet *hope for?* A very poor kind of faith we think that, which would give God credit for being *faithful*, when he had *performed his promises*! What! Believe what your senses cannot refute—things *accomplished*! Believe that which all history would condemn a man in not receiving! Is this *faith?* Our ideas of faith are, that it brings *distant* objects near! Things *distant* in the *future* —not so much in the *past*, which history renders *indisputable*! This is what we believe requires the exercise of faith 'Unfulfilled prophecy' was not given to *minister* to our faith at all, for it presupposes the reader to have entire faith in God.   It was given as Peter says, to be 'a light shining in a dark place'—to enlighten us with respect to the future.   A lantern unto which we do *ill* to take no heed as yet; but *well* if we will take hold of it, and be content to walk humbly with God in the light of his Word Millenarianism again here is seen, we think, to be *preeminently* the advocate of the Bible!   Should it be objected however, that many *Anti*-Millenarians are at one with us here, we reply by asking—is not this *another* phasis of the '*important service Millenarians have rendered to the Church*'?

THIRD. '*Anti*-Millenarians often tell us that the '*Personal* reign of Christ upon the earth,' with his saints would be derogatory to him.' Mr. Lyon expresses himself in sentiments somewhat similar. The question about the '*Personal* reign,' is not for man in his puny mind to settle, but to ascertain what saith the Scriptures concerning it   It is indeed appalling to hear sometimes from *Anti*-Millenarian pulpits this subject touched upon—the writer himself has heard again and

again men say—'We dont want Christ's *personal* presence'! Surely if such men
would consider the daring presumption of such expressions, they would cease for
ever to mention the subject again. Man presume in God's presence to state what
he *wants*, or does *not want*, upon such a theme—how awfully sad! But the ideas
men generally have about 'Christ's *personal* reign,' are as false as their conceptions of it are beclouded; they are in the bulk grounded upon *prejudice* and
man, instead of *faith* and *God*. When he comes we must not view him as the
suffering Saviour, but the *glorified* Redeemer! When he comes it will be in the
glory of the Father and of the Holy Angels—to gather out of his kingdom (before
his reign) all things that offend, and them which do iniquity! When he comes
he will fill the earth with his glory—banish the Devil and sin—bring about the
restitution of all things—give birth to that era—for which all creation, animate
and inanimate, rational and irrational—now groans and travails in pain, that
era when the Sons of God shall be manifested—when the nations shall fear
the name of the Lord, and all the kings of the earth his glory, yea, 'when the
Lord shall build up Zion, *he shall appear in his glory*'! And will all this be *derogatory* to him? Did that gleam of the coming kingdom which he gave his
disciples when he was transfigured, seem to convey any such idea? Was that
peep we say, of 'the Son of Man *coming* in his kingdom'—'the kingdom of God
come with power,' as seen in the Mount—that scene of which Peter speaks (2
Peter i. 16-21) "We saw the coming of the Lord Jesus Christ *in power* (not *in
person*, because he was there *personally* already so his coming spoken of in so
many places cannot be *spiritual*, because he is *spiritually* here *already*,—the context will always decide the nature of the coming spoken of,) and were eye-wit-
nesses of his *Majesty*, when we were with him in the holy Mount." This
dazzling manifestation we think, was but an earnest of his future 'kingdom of
glory.' Moses might be said to typify the dead saints who shall rise in the
*Pre*millennial resurrection; Elijah the living saints who shall not undergo death
only be changed,—but Christ himself the king in his beauty—in his *Majesty*, as
Peter says, now 'King of Kings and Lord of Lords' And will such be *derogatory* to him? What! did he get *glory* in his humiliation, and shall he not in
his future triumph? Did he get glory in his *incarnation* and *habitation* with
men in sinful flesh and shall not his '*personal* reign on the earth,' with those redeemed out of every kindred, and tongue, and people, and nation, bring glory too
at his return? How can Mr. Lyon say so, when he expresses himself as believing that *after* the Millennial era, *this earth* will be the abode of renewed

humanity, and if I mistake not like Dr. Brown—the abode specially of Christ too?
It is not the inspired account of the 'personal reign'   nor the creed of any Millenarian which have put such futile and silly notions into the minds of men. but
they are, we believe, the fruit of their own mistaken notions of Scripture truth
upon the subject, and their ignorance of the Millenarian exposition of the same !
They have been taught to believe from childhood, that the earth will continue
as it is until the end of time—saturated with sin and they carry with their
ideas into that future age, all the associations of sin and fallen humanity; they
measure themselves in the *future*, by themselves in the *present*; the earth in the
future, by the earth in the *present* and thus by confounding sin with holiness,
a mixture of tares and wheat with the pure grain refined, they are led into this
gross mistake in their conceptions of the future reign ! If such would consider
the scriptural declarations—that, death will then be swallowed up in victory—all
tears wiped away—no more sorrow or crying, because those things which produce sorrow—which bring forth tears, which cause pain, will then be expunged,
'the former things passed away'; if they would consider the vast physical
changes of the earth—the seasons lovely—the earth fruitful — barrenness changed
into fertility—the ploughman overtaking the reaper—the treader of grapes him
that soweth seed--the mountains (symbolically) dropping down new wine—the
earth yielding spontaneously her increase—the solitary places made glad, and the
desert blossoming as the rose . if they would consider the vast alteration in the
whole creation now groaning and seeking to be delivered from the bondage of
corruption, and set free into the *glorious* liberty of the children of God, when they
shall be manifested as Paul speaks of in his 8th chapter of the Romans,—that is
when their *body* shall be redeemed, we think such delusive and visionary ideas
of the 'personal reign' would *at once vanish* !

Talk of the earth as it will be after its new birth, being *derogatory* as an habitation! Can such men think for one moment *who* made it? Was it not pro-
nounced very good? What mean they then by talking about its being *derogatory*
as an habitation? They surely forget the Divine visits made to it *prior* to its
being cursed; and cannot allow their thoughts to wander upon the Divine being
who *walked* upon it for 33 years *after* it was *cursed*, when they talk about being
derogatory, but we say let God be the judge here, and let man be confounded and
ashamed. Paul says at the inspiration of the Spirit, 'For we know that the
whole creation groaneth and travaileth in pain together until now . and not only
they but *ourselves* also *which have the first-fruits of the spirit*, even we ourselves

groan within ourselves, waiting for the adoption, to wit—*the redemption of our body*" And John speaking of this selfsame era, says respecting the redeemed in soul and in body out of every kindred and tongue, and people and nation--"Thou hast made us unto our God kings and priests and we shall reign.. *where?*—among the stars? No! we shall reign *on the earth*! Heaven is a *state* and not a *place*, and may be *on the earth*, as well as anywhere else; where Christ is, *there is heaven*. Let those who view Christ's '*personal* reign *on the earth*' as derogatory, continue to do so,—we say the witness of God is *greater*—we will hold on 'to the law and to the testimony' And we might ask here whether Millenarian faith does not seem to be more praiseworthy than that which pretends to know better than John, and straightway goes to make his words speak something else more congenial to *man's own puny mind?*

FOURTH '*Anti*-Millenarians say, that as the Jews looked for a *carnal* instead of a *spiritual* kingdom so we are running into the same error, by expecting 'a *personal* reign of Christ *on the earth*, instead of his *spiritual* reign *in the hearts of men*' This proposition has the fallacy evident at first sight of confounding the future coming of Christ *in person*, with his presence *spiritually* here *now*! Before these passages teaching a *future* coming in glory *and in person*, can be turned into *spiritual* visitations, it is necessary that the *spirit* of Christ with his church in the world now for 1800 years *be withdrawn*! And moreover the same ideas we have been speaking of in our former proposition here again show themselves, present things tainted with sin, mixed up with that future reign, and the silly notion that *material* things are opposed to *spiritual* things! We might ask such, how they reconcile the fact of the *body* and the *soul* being at first united 'with God's *love* and *wisdom*! *Material, visible*, and *tangible* things are not opposed to *spiritual, unseen*, and *intangible* things, any further than they are tainted with sin; and when sin shall be banished, man and the material purified, rather than being *antagonistic*, they will become *mutual helpers* in the happiness of God's creatures! It is because of this strange unscriptural idea, that multitudes have overlooked entirely the '*resurrection* of the *body*,' disconnected entirely mind and matter, and made the believer to enter *at death*, upon the full enjoyment of bliss; instead of seeing its perfection *only* when the body and the soul shall again become united! Take away this modern delusion, and we see the reason of so little being said about *death* by the Apostles! We see here, I say, the reason why they placed before their followers so frequently the 'coming of the Lord,' as the reason preeminently for *watchfulness*, and not the *unnatural* article—*death*! How different the modern exhortations 'to watch'? 'Death—*always,* 'the coming of the Lord'—*never*! Nay, to make the Apostolic mode fit with the modern, 'the *Coming of the Lord,*' is now generally made to mean *death*! How strikingly hereby have we manifested the power of tradition grounded upon a false notion of God's inspired Word! Did Paul say he looked for his reward *at death?* "Henceforth there is laid up for me a crown of righteousness, which the Lord the righteous judge shall give me at '*that day,*' and not to me only, but unto all them that love '*his appearing,*'" "When the chief shepherd '*shall appear,*' ye shall receive a crown of glory that fadeth not away." So again Paul represents the 'Saviour's *appearing*' and *kingdom* as contemporaneous. In fact throughout Scripture teaches that the Saints' reward *in full* will be at the 'resurrection of the *body*'—when mind and matter shall again become united,—when Christ shall appear the second time, and not as is so very commonly supposed *at death!* And this is one great reason why the Saviour's return, in scripture holds such a prominent place—it was because of this that the Apostles 'and the early Christians were so anxious in their expectations for that 'blessed hope' as Paul calls it! So that the idea of separating what is *material,* from that which is *spiritual,* instead of getting any countenance from the Word of God, is crushed and crumbled without one exception! The Jewish error was in their carnally *depraved* views of that kingdom, and not in their idea of Christ's *personal* reign; and so far they present a striking *analogy* to the majority of *Anti-*Materialists now! They looked indeed for the *immediate* appearance of that kingdom, and were wrong in point of *time,* although right in point of *fact ,*—they wanted the crown without the cross—the kingdom of glory without the kingdom of grace preparatory to it. But, perhaps, an *Anti-*Materialist objector might here step forward with such texts as these, which *Anti-*Millenarians are so fond of talking about— "My kingdom is not of *this world,* if my kingdom were of *this world* then would my servants fight, that I should not be delivered to the Jews, but now is my kingdom *not from hence,*" This text is brought forward until it is threadbare, to prove the fallacy of a '*personal* reign.' Now let any intelligent mind consider it for one moment, and then tell us whether it will serve any such purpose. In what sense is '*his* kingdom' herein said to be '*not of this world*'? Is it because of its *immateriality?* because it is opposed to *matter?* or will not every intelligent mind say—it was because it was opposed to the '*sinful depraved* customs of *this world?* It was because '*his* kingdom' had not those accursed principles that engender war and strife and not because of its being opposed to *matter,* that he said

L

—"If my kingdom were of this world (like unregenerate men) then would my servants *fight*"! He ought not here to have talked about having a kingdom at all as yet, to meet the requirements of *Anti*-Millenarians. His *spiritual* kingdom was *then* begun. '*My* kingdom'—teaches that he had *then* a kingdom. What meaneth the phrase then—'Now is my kingdom not *from hence*'? not as yet *begun*—not from *this* time? Could '*not from hence,*' refer to what he had *then?* or did it not refer to that kingdom of Daniel's—*yet to be set up?* We unhesitatingly affirm the latter, and this very text instead of establishing the views of those who profess to be entire *spiritualists*, refutes the same and points like the rest of scripture to that kingdom which will be characterized not only for its *spirituality*, but its *materiality* too! Again, such texts as these are perverted in the same way to make them speak what they were never intended—"Ye are not of the world, therefore the world hateth you" The plain surface meaning is as palpably evident as words could possibly make it. Ye are not after the *sinful* —*fallen*—*depraved* manner of this world, and because of this, you suffer persecution—*therefore* the world hateth you. Instead therefore of running in error here, the Millenarian hold all the blessings of the gospel day and *spiritual* kingdom as well as the *Anti*-Millenarian, and expects yet a brighter and better world in point of *spirituality* and *materiality* too· while the *Anti*-Millenarian glides along in his visionary ideas of '*no materiality,*' until he falls into a mixed Millennium little if anything better than the present, which he takes to *himself* the credit in some very considerable measure of making, and makes out consequently in the end that his kingdom of *spiritualities*, for which he has been contending is essentially carnal and mixed up with the *material* world, in its present *cursed* and *sinful* state! which view appears the more honorable to God; which view appears the more ennobling to man? which view seems (apart from Scripture evidence) to be more in accordance with what we would deem purely—*Spiritual?*

FIFTH. Millenarianism is essentially founded upon the atonement of Christ, and the inspiration of the Scriptures, and its practical tendency is to spread Evangelical Religion. Mr. Lyon here confronts us with his '*Millenarian incongruity,*' and says we look for Christ daily to put an end to the present state of things, so that we cut away the possibility of evangelizing the world: and not only so, but actually present the '*incongruity*' of the foundation of the 'spiritual temple,' requiring 4,000 *years* to lay it, while the Temple itself is raised upon that foundation in less than *half that space of time*! Upon the first part of this accusation we only observe, that Mr. Lyon's view places him in such a position that the world's population *never* can be evangelized, while upon the Millenarian view of Scripture, a foundation for it is laid in its widest sense. Mr. Lyon must make *bright* prophetic pictures mean *obscure* ones, *universal* mean *partial*,—*all* know the Lord from the *least to the greatest*—mean that—'*vast numbers* will be but Christian in name'; and so by *lowering* the standard of the Millennium to make it fit with the wheat and tares growing together, &c. &c., he *excludes* the possibility of the world's future history, being *bright* as Scripture leads us to expect! Another specimen of Mr. Lyon's charges against Millenarianism, may be here noticed appropriately—he says, p, 123, "*Scripture* leads us to expect a time, when all nations whom God has made, shall come and worship before him." '*Millenarianism* leads us to the conclusion, that all nations shall soon be destroyed by the fires of the final day'! '*Christ's last command*, leads us to expect a time, when the gospel shall be carried into all the world, and preached to every creature'. *Millenarianism* precludes the possibility of this, by virtually sweeping the race of men away long before this command has been fulfilled!" Mr. Lyon can have the choice of two things—either pleading as an excuse for these statements—his ignorance of the views of men, he has essayed to criticise: or stand charged with 'a wilful misrepresentation of what he knew to be their views. Really such *caricatures* require no ordinary amount of self-restraint to avoid dealing with them as they deserve. Whatever may be the difference of opinion among Millenarians respecting the conflagration, they one and all believe in the entire fulfilment of God's promises, respecting the world's conversion—both as regards Jews and Heathen, either before the Second Advent, or as the accompaniments of it. Not as Mr. Lyon says—"because the Spirit *fails* in 2,000 years to effect this work"; but because such is *God's revealed will*! Mr. Lyon might with equal propriety talk about, 'the Spirit having at present *failed* to effect this work! But we would here make an observation or two upon the *practical tendency* of the means employed by modern controversialists, to forward the two views. And this we would indeed gladly avoid, did not the value of inspiration in these days of scepticism rise superior to everything else. We ask, is it not a fact that our *Anti*-Millenarian brethren are now seeking out '*contradictions*' in prophecy to set aside the *Pre*-Millennial Advent? Is it not a fact that that they are now attempting to show the *literal* fulfilment impossible, because of seeming '*contradictions*' and '*discrepancies*'? Is it not a fact that they are now attempting to found their *allegorical* interpretations upon passages of Scripture, by showing their *literal* acceptation, to involve either a '*con-

tradiction' or a *discrepancy?*   Mr. Lyon, we think, made a fearful mistake, when he sought to help out his theory by telling us Mr. F. W. Newman derived an argument against inspiration, from the views of his ancestors or friends, who he says were Millenarians. What! could he be so blind as to shut his eyes against the surging torrent of *Anti*-inspirationism now flowing from his *own side* and likely to deluge the land? Could he be so blind as not to see this when he wrote so *incautiously?* Could he not see that the very arguments he himself in common with other *Anti*-Millenarians are using, are only preparing a *'means of attack'* for those who deny the inspiration of the Scriptures ? What we may ask more calculated to *undermine* inspiration, than publishing—*'Prophetical contradictions?'* What more likely to help the Sceptic than publishing *'discrepancies'* between Prophets and Apostles ? Will Infidelity, Scepticism, and *Anti*-inspirationism not smile at these things ? Let our *Anti*-Millenarian brethren be granted the premises they are now seeking—*'a contradiction'* between inspired writers or *'a discrepancy'* between the respective accounts of these writers or that these accounts are *literally irreconcilable,*—and what then will be the *practical advantage gained?* Why it is upon this foundation, and by these selfsame arguments, that infidels, sceptics, and the opponents of inspiration, always have, and are now taking their stand! We are sorry to have to write thus, but surely our brethren are heedless as to consequences! Surely if *Anti*-Millenarianism has got no practical advantage, the *'means employed'* to spread it have *less !* !

SIXTH. 'Anti-Millenarians often say that it does not matter, after all, whether we trouble ourselves about the *how* or *when* of the Coming of Christ, provided we are resting upon him for salvation.' Can such a system, producing such a sluggish and unhealthy state of feeling in the christian world, be regarded as sound? This state of things is seen in the present day, to manifest itself in a variety of forms. If the subject of the Second Advent be introduced, the person introducing such subject will very often be met with something like this —"We have seen or heard many 'Lo heres and lo theres, see heres and see theres' come to nought in our day," that is as much as to say, because some have abused the doctrine of the Second Advent, they will have nothing to say or think upon it. How sad that Scripture should be taken up and perverted thus. When our Lord uttered these words, with the command—'Go not after them nor follow them,' it was to show us *the certainty* of his Second Coming, rather than teach us to *ignore* it ! They were spoken to show the utter folly of listening to any *local* pretender ; for his coming would be ' as the lightning that

lighteneth out of the one under heaven and shineth unto the other part under
heaven, even so should the Coming of the Son of Man be." not a *local* or circumscribed event, but a *universal* manifestation!   Again, with others there is
a kind of fear, a timidity or dread even to read a book upon the subject. Present
a Work to a lady, perhaps otherwise, well instructed in evangelical principles,
and she will look upon your request, to read it, as unfriendly; thinking that you
are thereby going to place before her, out of God's '*revealed things*,' some of his
'*awful secrets*!'   "*Secret* things (I am informed she adds) belong unto God,'
(forgetting, of course, as is usually done, to add the rest of the sentence) but
things that are *revealed* (the entire Bible) belong unto us and to our children
for ever, that we may do all the words of this law."   Then again, is it not a fact
that, among the masses of our congregations, the idea of the return of the Lord
at all, is either *entirely* or well nigh banished from their minds, if perchance *it
ever found an entrance there?* May not the lamentable state of the christian world,
upon this point, be traced to the evil tendency of that system which teaches that we
have, at least, *a thousand years yet* to calculate on, before he *can come?* But
Christ has specially foretold this state of things as *characterizing* the time when
he should appear!   Part of the *professing* church, he says, will slumber and
sleep, instead of being vigilant.   'While the bridegroom tarried they all
slumbered and slept, and at midnight, when the cry is made—Behold the bridegroom cometh, go ye out to meet him.   It is said five were *wise* and five were
foolish.   The *foolish* had no oil—their lamps not trimmed; they were not, in
fact, *on the look-out* for the bridegroom!   Ah! we need not ask here which is
the *wise* view—that of looking for Christ at *any* day, or that of looking for a
'*defined thousand years*' yet to intervene between the present and his Advent!
The *practical tendency* of the two views, we think, will not admit of any comparison in the light of Scripture   The one seems to swell with importance while
we think of it, while the other sinks down into the drowsy state of the foolish
virgins —'My Lord delayeth his Coming'—he *cannot* come for *a thousand years
yet*!   Ah, yes! to put the question of right or wrong altogether aside, we think
the *practical tendency* of the two views will not admit of any comparison.   Our
incitements to watchfulness must be incalculably greater than theirs.   The
privileges we hold as laid up for the Saints at the revelation of Christ from
heaven, at his *Pre*-Millenial Advent, are vastly greater than theirs.   The
stimulus we have to work while it is called to-day, as we contemplate the fact
of his Advent drawing nearer and nearer, must be tenfold greater than theirs;

and when we come to consider that should we after all be mistaken, that we '*lose nothing*,' while, on the other hand, should our brethren be mistaken and surprised anon with the cry 'Behold the bridegroom *is here*,' what untold importance does the consideration not lend to the former, who must be safe at *all hazards;* while the latter, to say the least, *may be wrong*, and in the drowsy state consequent upon looking for *a thousand years yet to elapse*, hear his Lord say, as he had occasion once, in the days of his flesh—'What could ye not watch *for* me one hour?' Did I not tell you I should come *suddenly, unexpectedly*, 'even as a thief in the night?' Did I not exhort you to watch *therefore?* Yea, we are told that some will enter in, being found ready, '*watching*,' while to others *the door will be shut*!

May we be found '*watching*,' '*waiting*' and ready, should he appear in our day ; if not may it be our privilege to rise with his redeemed family, and share with Paul in that *first* and *better* resurrection, to attain which he was so anxious and strove so hard !

ALLNUTT & CO , PRINTERS, BEACONSFIELD.

www.ingramcontent.com/pod-product-compliance
Lightning Source LLC
Chambersburg PA
CBHW081519040426
42447CB00013B/3277